AN EXPOSE' OF THE ADVERSARY

GARRY D. PIFER

Copyright © 2023 by Garry D. Pifer

All rights reserved in accordance with the U. S. Copyright Act of 1978, the scanning, uploading, and electronic sharing of any part of this book without the permission of the author is unlawful piracy and theft of the author's intellectual property. If you would like to use material from the book, prior written permission must be obtained by contacting the author.

ISBN	978-1-7353332-9-8 (paperback)
ISBN	979-8-9895556-0-4 (ebook)
Library of Congress Control No	2023923028

Unless otherwise noted, Scriptures are taken from the King James Version of the Bible, KJV.

Other Scripture quotations taken from the following:

International Standard Version, ISV, Copyright © 2011 by the ISV Foundation, Bradenton, FL Used by permission.

The Peshitta: The Holy Bible From the Ancient Eastern Text – The Holy Bible as translated directly from the Aramaic (Syrian) Text by Scholar George M. Lamsa (1892-1975). Originally published by A. J. Holman Co. For information contact HarperCollins Publishers, N. Y., NY.

Brenton Septuagint Translation, translator Lancelot Charles Lee Brenton (1807-1862). Originally published 1851. In public domain.

Young's Literal Translation, YLT, translation made by Robert Young (1822-1888), published in 1862. In public domain.

The Bible in Basic English, BBE, a translation of the Bible into basic English by Professor S. H. Hooke. The New Testament was released in 1941 and the Old Testament in 1949, In public domain.

James Moffatt Bible, 1926, Kregel Publications, 2450 Oak Industrial Dr. NE, Grand Rapids, MI 49505

Revised Standard Version (RSV), 1952, Published by National Council of the Churches of Christ

    110 Maryland Ave. Suite 108

    Washington, DC 20002

New Revised Standard Version (NRSV), 1989, Published by National Council of the Churches of Christ

    110 Maryland Ave. Suite 108

    Washington, DC 20002

Weymouth New Testament, 1903 and 1912, in the public domain.

Concordant Version of the Old Testament, 1926, Concordant Publishing Concern

    P.O. Box 449

    Almont, MI 48003

The New American Bible, 1987, revised 2010, Catholic Book Publishing Corp.

    77 West End Road

    Totowa, NJ 07512

    Douay Confraternity Bible, 1941, Catholic Book Publishing Corp., 77 West End Road, Totowa, NJ

    07512

Good News Translation (GNT), formerly called the *Good News Bible,* 2nd edition 1992,

American Bible Society
101 N. Independence Mall East, FL. 8
Philadelphia, PA 19106
Definitions and comments marked as follows:
Strong's Exhaustive Concordance of the Bible by James Strong, Copyright © 2009 by Thomas Nelson, Nashville, TN.
Thayer's Greek-English Lexicon of the New Testament by Joseph Henry Thayer. Copyright © 1996 by Hendrickson Publishers, Peabody, MA.
Vine's Expository Dictionary of Biblical Words by editors W. E. Vine, Merrill F. Unger, William White Jr. Copyright © 1985 by Thomas Nelson, Inc., Publishers, Nashville, TN.
A Hebrew and English Lexicon of the Old Testament first published in 1906 by F. Brown, S. Driver, C. Briggs (BDB), In public domain.
Davis Dictionary of the Bible by John D. Davis. Copyright © 1924. Reprinted by Baker Book House under special arrangement with the Board of Christian Education of the Presbyterian Church in the United States of America.
Third College Edition Websters (New World Dictionary) ® of American English. Copyright © 1994 by Simon & Schuster, Inc., a Paramount Communications Company.
The Companion Bible, Dr. E. W. Bullinger 1906-1922, Kregel Publications
2450 Oak Industrial Dr. NE
Grand Rapids, MI 49505
Adam Clarke's Commentary of the Bible, originally published 1810, © 1967 Beacon Hill Press

Barnes' Notes on the Whole Bible, 1832, In public domain.
John Wesley's Explanatory Notes of the Whole Bible, 1754-1765, In public domain.
Matthew Henry's Commentary on the Whole Bible, 1706, In public domain.
Jamieson-Fausset-Brown Bible Commentary, 1871, In public domain.

Any Internet addresses (websites, blogs, emails, etc.) and telephone numbers in this book are offered as a resource. They are not intended in any way to be or imply an endorsement by the author, nor does the author vouch for the content of these sites and numbers for the life of this book.

Interior design: www.fiverr.com freelance services

Cover design: www.fiverr.com freelance services

Cover image: Licensed stock images

Proofreader/editor: Anna Hagen

Printed in the United States of America   Published at Edmonton, KY

gdpifer@scrtc.com

And the great dragon was cast out, that old serpent, called the devil, and satan, which deceiveth the whole world:

(Rev. 12:9)

DEDICATION

One Fall about 20 years ago a number of families, friends and friends of friends, spent a week together at a large home that had been turned into an Executive Retreat. Our religious backgrounds were similar and we enjoyed the special fellowship and time together. We were from 7 different states and of varying ages, some with small children and some with grown children. One of the highlights was spending time in Bible study. One day Andrea, from Colorado, made a statement that was contrary to anything I had ever heard. She said that Lucifer, which I had always been told was a name for the devil, was not the devil at all. She explained that Lucifer was a Latin word that wasn't a proper name for anyone or anything. A seed had been planted and over the following months and years I studied what the Bible really said about this being, the devil, the adversary. This book contains much of what I discovered. I wish to dedicate the book to Andrea, thankful for the seed she planted.

CONTENTS

INTRODUCTION	1
LUCIFER IS NOT SATAN!	5
PRINCE OF TYRUS	17
THE SATAN OF THE BIBLE	29
"GET THEE BEHIND ME, SATAN"	46
LUKE 10:18 I BEHELD SATAN...	49
THE ANGELS THAT SINNED	53
ORIGIN AND PURPOSE OF THE ADVERSARY	65
THE BEGINNING OF THE SERPENT	74
YOU AND ME AND THE ADVERSARY	87
ABOUT THE AUTHOR	93
OTHER BOOKS BY GARRY D. PIFER	94

INTRODUCTION

"Stunningly, Americans are more confident about the existence of Satan than they are of God. Overall, 56% contend that Satan is an influential spiritual being, yet almost half (49%) are not fully confident that God truly exists."[1] (Cultural Research Center, Arizona Christian University) Although Americans predominantly claim to be "Christians" it seems many don't believe in a devil. Further those who do claim to believe don't know exactly who or what he is. I found the results of a poll the Barna Group did in 2009. Posted on the website *barna.com*[2] was the following. "Four out of ten Christians (40%) strongly agreed that Satan 'is not a living being but is a symbol of evil'. An additional two out of ten Christians (19%) said they 'agree somewhat' with that perspective."

The Encyclopedia Britannica under the heading of "Devil"[3] gives us the following. "In the monotheistic Western religions, the Devil is viewed as a fallen angel who in pride has tried to usurp the position of the one and only God. In Judaism and, later, Christianity, the Devil

---

[1] Arizona Christian University Cultural Research Center George Barna, director of research
https://www.arizonachristian.edu/wp-content/uploads/2020/04/CRC-AWVI-2020-Release-03_Perceptions-of-God.pdf
[2] https://www.barna.com/research/most-american-christians-do-not-believe-that-satan-or-the-holy-spirit-exist/
[3] Encyclopedia Britannica "Devil" published May 11, 2023
https://www.britannica.com/topic/devil

was known as Satan. In the Old Testament, Satan is viewed as the prosecutor of Yahweh's court, as in Job, chapters 1 and 2, but he is not regarded as an adversary of God. In postbiblical Judaism and in Christianity, however, Satan became known as the 'prince of devils' and assumed various names: Beelzebub ('Lord of Flies') in Matthew 12:24-27, often cited as Beelzebul ('Lord of Dung'), and Lucifer (the fallen angel of light)."

It appears that even among those who claim to believe in a devil there are a number of beliefs and concepts. You can search out many of these concepts on the internet. Due to various artists' renderings and depictions in plays from the middle ages most, it seems, view the devil as an ugly goat- like creature with horns, a tail, and a pitchfork. Most picture him (and most believe the devil to be a male) wearing a red outfit, although at one time he was portrayed as being blue or in blue.

One almost universal belief is that the devil was once an archangel, named Lucifer. It is believed that he became quite lifted up in pride and attempted to usurp God's position and authority. He, according to this belief, managed to convince a full third of God's angels to join him in his rebellion. This, according to the story, resulted in a major war of the good angels against the "fallen" angels. He, consequentially, was cast out of heaven and banished to the earth. And, he was there waiting, to throw a massive "monkey wrench" into God's plan when He created mankind. In this book we will look at this belief and at the Scripture that supposedly proves this belief to be true. We will also look at many of the other beliefs and views that are held by the vast majority of Christians.

The belief outlined above was first put forward by two of the early "church fathers," Tertullian and Origen. The following is taken from an article by a Bible teacher from the U.K., Julian Spriggs.[4]

"Tertullian (160-220) was the first of the church fathers who taught that Satan was a fallen angel, by quoting Ezekiel 28 (Against Marcion 2:10). Origen (c.185-c.254) also quoted Isaiah 14, Ezekiel 28 and Luke 10:18 to teach that Satan, or Lucifer, had fallen from glory in heaven (De Principis 1:5:5, Against Celsus 6:44). Although rejected by the Reformers, this teaching was popularized through Milton's vivid description of Satan's rebellion and fall in Book I of 'Paradise Lost', and now, at least on a popular level in the church, seems to be accepted without being questioned."

As we proceed through this book we will discover that most of what is taught and believed is not true or accurate according to the Bible. And, that shouldn't really surprise or shock us. After all the devil is a liar and the father of all lies. (John 8:44) We are also told that he has deceived the whole world. (Rev. 12:9) He would like nothing better than to have us believing his lies and fabrications as to who and what he is.

---

[4] Julian Spriggs https://www.julianspriggs.co.uk/pages/FallOfSatan

CHAPTER ONE

LUCIFER IS NOT SATAN!

I've been taught throughout my lifetime that the being we refer to as the devil was once an archangel named Lucifer and that he rebelled against God and became "Satan." Where did that teaching come from? Most of you will respond by telling me that Isaiah 14 reveals that to us. Does this chapter really teach us that? Does it support that teaching? Let us look at this chapter and see if it really reveals that.

COMMENTARIES

Before we turn to the Scriptures, let us look at what some of the well known Bible commentaries tell us. First from Adam Clarke's commentary on Isaiah 14:12.

"Verse 12. O Lucifer, son of the morning] The Versions in general agree in this translation, and render *heilel* as signifying Lucifer, the morning star, whether Jupiter or Venus; as these are both bringers of the morning light, or morning stars, annually in their turn. And although the context speaks explicitly concerning Nebuchadnezzar, yet this has been, I know not why, applied to the chief of the fallen angels, who is most incongruously denominated Lucifer, (the bringer of light!) an epithet as common to him as those of Satan and Devil. That the Holy Spirit by his prophets should call this arch-enemy of God and man the light-bringer, would be strange indeed. But the truth is, the text speaks nothing at all concerning Satan nor his fall, nor the occasion of that fall, which many divines have with great confidence deduced from this text. O how necessary it is to understand the literal meaning of Scripture, that preposterous comments may be prevented! Besides, I doubt whether our translation be correct. *heilel*, which we translate Lucifer, comes from *yalal,* yell, howl or shriek, and should be translated, 'Howl, son of the morning;' and so the Syriac has understood it; and for this meaning Michaelis contends: see his reasons in Parkhurst, under *halal.*"

Let us look further at John Wesley's comments in his commentary of Isaiah 14:12.

"Fallen - From the height of thy glory. Lucifer - Which properly is a bright star, that ushers in the morning; but is here metaphorically taken for the mighty king of Babylon. Son - The title of son is given in scripture not only to a person or thing begotten or produced by another, but also to any thing which is related, to it, in which sense we read of the son of a night, Jonah 4:10, a son of perdition, John 17:12, and, which is more agreeable, to the present case, the sons of Arcturus, Job 38:32."

And, from one more commentary, Matthew Henry's:

"How hast thou fallen from heaven, O Lucifer! son of the morning! v. 11, 12. The king of Babylon shone as brightly as the morning star, and fancied that wherever he came he brought day along with him; and has such an illustrious prince as this fallen, such a star become a clod of clay? Did ever any man fall from such a height of honour and power into such an abyss of shame and misery? This has been commonly alluded to (and it is a mere allusion) to illustrate the fall of the angels...."

Isaiah 14

Just reading these commentators' words I think we have to begin to question the teaching we have grown up with. So, let us begin our study by looking briefly at the verses in question in Isaiah 14.

"How art thou fallen from heaven, O Lucifer, son of the morning! [how] art thou cut down to the ground, which didst weaken the nations! For thou hast said in thine heart, I will ascend into heaven, I will exalt my throne above the stars of God: I will sit also upon the mount of the congregation, in the sides of the north: I will ascend above the heights of the clouds; I will be like the most High." (Isa. 14:12-14)

Let us first notice who God is addressing Himself to in this passage of Scripture. Verse 4, "That thou shall take up this proverb against the king of Babylon..." God is speaking of and to and about "the King of Babylon," not Lucifer, not "Satan", not a cherub. Drop down a few verses and we will see that God tells us of the end of this man's reign, verse 11. "Thy (referring to the king of Babylon) pomp is brought down to the grave, ("Satan" never died or was placed into a grave) and the noise of thy viols (harps or lutes): the worm (or maggots) is spread under thee (maggots do not eat spirit bodies), and the worms cover thee."

Your teaching and mine have been much alike and you are probably already parroting the old line, "but the narrative jumps in verse 12 from the king of Babylon to the spirit being named Lucifer". Does it? Is this "Lucifer" of verse 12 "Satan" the devil? What does the end of the king of Babylon, in verse 11, have to do with the beginning of "Satan"?

Let us look at verse 12 again. "How art thou fallen from heaven, O Lucifer, son of the morning! [how] art thou cut down to the ground, which didst weaken the nations!" We need to understand. Notice again what we read in verse 4 that God says to take up this proverb against the "king of Babylon." Picking up this "proverb" in verse 10, which is after all the "trees" (different people which feared the king), spoken of in verses 6-8, are at rest because of the king's demise. We will see if this "Lucifer theory" fits into these verses without twisting and wresting the English language.

Verses 10-14 of Isaiah 14, "All they shall speak and say unto thee (king of Babylon), art thou (king of Babylon) also become weak as we? art thou (king of Babylon) become like unto us (mortal men and not gods from heaven)? Thy (king of Babylon) pomp is brought down to the grave, [and] the noise of thy (king of Babylon) viols; the worm is spread under thee (king of Babylon), and the worms cover thee (king of Babylon). How art thou (king of Babylon) fallen from heaven, O Lucifer..." Okay, what is this? How can the king of Babylon, the king of Babylon, the king of Babylon, the king of Babylon, the king of Babylon, the king of Babylon, the king of Babylon, the king of Babylon (made reference to eight times in two sentences), suddenly turn into "Lucifer" in the middle of a sentence? Is "Lucifer" a proper name? Is

"Lucifer" another name for the king of Babylon? Is "Lucifer" an English word? Is there a Hebrew word that can be translated "Lucifer?"

LUCIFER

Doing a bit of research we find that this word "Lucifer" appears NO other place in all of Scripture. Furthermore, "Lucifer" is not a Hebrew word, nor is it an English translation of a Hebrew word. "Lucifer" is Latin! And, it is related to a group of Latin derived English words including lucid, luciferin, and luciferose. All of these words suggest brightness or shining. "Lucifer" is the Latin Vulgate translation of the word "*xosphoruos*" in the Septuagint. This Greek word "*xosphoruos*" is the root of the English words fluorescence and phosphorescence. They also suggest brightness and shining.

Interestingly, there are no Hebrew or Aramaic texts in which there is a word in this verse that corresponds. What is found in ALL such texts is the word "*hehlehl*," "*eill*", which is a form of the Hebrew stem "*yah-iahl*," *ill*. And what is the meaning of "*ill*?" It means HOWL! So, where does this bring us? There appears to be some confusion between a word meaning "brightness" and one meaning "howl." It has been suggested that the translators of the Septuagint may have overlooked the smallest of the Hebrew letters or perhaps were using a copy in which it had been inadvertently omitted. Thus if the form of the word *eill*, as it occurs in this particular verse, were shortened to *ell* its meaning would be derived from a different root, in fact would be itself a different root, and the sense given in the Septuagint and the Vulgate would be at least understandable. However, there is still one gigantic exception. It could possibly mean "a shining one," but there is ABSOLUTELY NO reason or rule of grammar for turning the word into a personal name such as "Lucifer." Doubtless the King James Version translators followed the Vulgate as they did in most of their translating.

Following is a listing of all of the King James renderings of the word that is found in the "Hebrew" texts and transliterations of its various forms. Every occurrence in the entire King James Version is listed. You can be the judge. In ALL Hebrew or Aramaic texts of Isaiah 14:12 the only word found is "*heh-lehl*," *eill*, which is a form of the Hebrew stem "*yah-lahl*," *ill*, meaning howl. Here is Kittel's[5] Hebrew Text for the Hebrew stem ill–"*yah-lahl*"–HOWL:

Isa 13:6 *eiliu* Howl ye

Isa 14:31 *eili* Howl

Isa 15: *iilil* shall howl

Isa.15:3 *iilil* shall howl

Isa.16:7 *iilil* Howl

Isa.16:7 *iilil* shall howl

Isa. 23:1 *eililu* Howl ye

Isa. 23:6 *eililu* Howl ye

Isa. 23:14 *eilile* Howl ye

Isa. 52:5 *eililu* make to howl

Isa. 65:14 *eililu* shall howl

---

[5] Kittel, Rudolph German Old Testament scholar. He produced commentaries and histories of the Israelites and the near East but his most enduring work was his critical edition of the Hebrew Scriptures – Biblia Hebraica – which has remained a standard text.

Jer. 4:8 *ueililu* Howl

Jer. 25:34 *eililu* Howl

Jer. 47:2 *ueill* and shall howl

Jer. 48:20 *eilili* Howl

Jer. 48:31 *ailil* will I howl

Jer. 48:39 *eililu* They shall howl (Howl ye)

Jer. 49:3 *eilili* Howl (Howl ye)

Jer. 51:8 *eililu* howl

Ezek. 30:2 *eililu* Howl ye

Hos. 7:14 *ililu* They howled

Joel 1:5 *ueililu* And howl

Joel 1:11 *eililu* howl

Joel 1:13 *eililu* And shall be howlings

Amos 8:1 *ueililu* and howl

Micah 1:8 *uailile* howl ye

Zeph. 1:11 *aililu* Howl

Zech. 11:2 *eill* howl

Zech. 11:2 *eililu* howl

Isa. 14:12 *eill* LUCIFER (??)

One need not be a Hebrew scholar to see at once that "Lucifer" is totally out of place in this listing. The meaning of this word is exceedingly clear; *eill* is a verb that means "HOWL", and not a noun that can be in any way twisted into a personal name such as "Lucifer"!

Please notice carefully that the Hebrew verb *eill* in Isa. 14:12 is the very same identical form of the first verb *eill* in Zech. 11:2. Let us try substituting the personal noun "Lucifer" in place of the verb "howl" in the two places it occurs in Zech. 11:2. (Note that here as in many scriptures, the trees are likened to people who are crying out because of death and destruction.) "Lucifer, fir tree; for the cedar is fallen; because the mighty are spoiled: Lucifer, O ye oaks of Bashan; for the forest of the vintage is come down."

I think you will have to agree such a translation would be nonsense. Let us try the same substitution back in Isaiah 14 where we find the word Lucifer in verse 12. Notice how this word is translated in verse 31. Instead of "Howl, O gate; cry, O city..." We would have it read, "Lucifer, O gate; cry, O city..." Again, such a translation would be pure nonsense; just as it is also nonsense translated that way in Isa. 14:12.

In a footnote Kittel tells us that it is only in the Septuagint (which is the Greek Translation of the Hebrew Scriptures) that we find this word *ell* instead of *eill*. This word was translated into *eospearos*, which Jerome translated into Lucifer with a capital "L" and which the King James translators carried over into our English Bible without checking the HEBREW manuscripts. If they would have it would have solved this dilemma. ALL of the Hebrew manuscripts have *eill* in Isaiah 14:12. And, keep in mind that the Old Testament was written in Hebrew, NOT Greek or Latin.

Other translations

Let us read a few translations other than the King James Version and see how they have dealt with this strange word *ell* which comes to us by way of the Greek Septuagint and the Latin Vulgate.

"How you are fallen from heaven, O morning star, son of the dawn! You are hacked down to the earth, destroyer of nations." (New International Version)

"How you are fallen from heaven, O Day Star, son of Dawn! (New Revised Standard Version) Note: There is absolutely no reason to capitalize "day," "star," or "dawn" in this version.

A few translations have chosen to follow the Hebrew manuscripts rather than the Catholic Latin Bible. "How you have fallen from the heavens! Howl, son of the dawn! You are hacked down to the earth, defeater of all nations." (Concordant Literal Old Testament) "How are you fallen from heaven! howl in the morning! for you have fallen down to the ground, O reviler of the nations." (Holy Bible from the Ancient Eastern Text, George M. Lamsa's translation)

On an internet website that is designed as a resource for professors, theologians, and the like[6] I found something quite interesting. It was brought out that Jerome did translate the Hebrew word we are discussing as "Lucifer" but he stated in his commentary on Isaiah 14:12 that the word meant something else entirely. The English translation of his

---

[6] Biblical Hermeneutics Stack Exchange
https://hermeneutics.stackexchange.com/questions/20952/in-isaiah-1412-did-the-king-james-translator-make-a-mistake-using-the-term-luci

Latin commentary says, "In Hebrew, so that we may express it word-for-word, 'How have you fallen from heaven! Howl, son of the dawn'!"

FALLEN FROM HEAVEN

Another question that we need to address is just who was it that fell from heaven? And does the phrase "fallen from heaven" prove that this individual had to have been at God's throne or in heaven to "fall from heaven" therefore proving that this must have been a spirit being? The answer is NO. This is simply a figure of speech. And, to prove this, let us look to the words of our Savior in Luke 10:15. "And thou, Capernaum, which art exalted to heaven, shalt be thrust down to hell." So here we have a whole city being thrown down from heaven to hades, their grave. And so it is with the King of Babylon whose "pomp is brought down to the grave" (Isa. 14:11) These two scriptures have exact parallel thoughts.

From the context, it is very clear that it is the king of Babylon who elevated himself to high heaven in the heavens of his own mind, and it is the same king of Babylon who has "fallen from the heavens," and it is the same king of Babylon who is "hacked down to the earth," and it is the same king of Babylon who was the "defeater of all nations," and not a "perfect Satan."

Before we move on, let us look at verses 13 and 14 of Isaiah 14. Do we find any sign of "Satan" here? Isaiah 14:13, "For thou hast said in thine heart, I will ascend into heaven, I will exalt my throne above the stars of God: I will sit also upon the mount of the congregation, in the sides of the north:"

Isaiah 14:14, "I will ascend above the heights of the clouds; I will be like the most High.

Many would have us believe this is speaking of a spirit being rebelling against God and attempting to displace Him. As we have seen, the context has been about a man and a system. So, the language here shouldn't be a surprise. It is a continuation of Babylon, the same system that started at Babel, where they first thought to build "a tower whose top may reach into heaven." (Gen. 11:4)

Now verse 15, "Yet thou shalt be brought down to hell (*sheol*–the grave), to the sides of the pit (cistern, hole, dungeon, or possibly crypt)" This is speaking of the demise, the death, of the king of Babylon, not the death of "Satan".

Maybe there is some sign of "satan" in verse 16, "They that see thee (has any man seen "Satan"?) shall narrowly look (gaze) upon thee, [and] consider thee, [saying, Is] this the man ("man?" This is no "Satan" but a MAN!) that made the earth to tremble, that did shake kingdoms;"

As one continues reading there are more references to a "man," not a spirit being. Verse 19, "But thou art cast out of thy grave..." Verse 20, "Thou shalt not be joined with them in burial,..." We find in these verses that just like many of the Pharaohs and rulers of other nations who taught and thought that they were "gods" and who exalted themselves and their thrones to heaven, this king of Babylon was also just a MAN. And, God Almighty tells him to "HOWL" because He is going to bring him "DOWN TO HELL," (the grave.) And, from history and archaeology we find that is exactly what happened.

After looking at the context, understanding the unfortunate translation and capitalization used here, and without making assumptions, it is quite clear that there was no archangel named Lucifer that rebelled against God and became the adversary, called "Satan," being talked about here. Isaiah 14 is speaking only of a man, the king of Babylon, not an archangel.

CHAPTER TWO

PRINCE OF TYRUS

Ezekiel 28

Most of us have been told that the account of the Prince of Tyrus, found in Ezekiel 28, is a record of "Satan's fall" from a position of a perfect cherub. Let us look at this account in some detail and come to understand it.

But, before we turn to chapter 28, let us notice the whole context here. This all begins back in chapter 26. Verse 2, "Son of man, because that Tyrus hath said..." Verse 3, "Therefore thus saith the Lord God; Behold, I am against thee, O Tyrus..." Verse 4 speaks of Tyrus and also verse 7. This whole chapter is a prophecy about the destruction of the city of Tyrus, or Tyre. We know from history that it happened as God prophesied. Chapter 27 continues with a lamentation against Tyrus, verse 2. A lamentation is defined as a "funeral dirge." So, when we come to chapter 28 the context continues with the subject of Tyrus, this time addressed to the leader, the "prince" or "king."

Chapter 28 and verse 2, "Son of man, say unto the prince of Tyrus, Thus saith the Lord God, Because thine heart is lifted up, and thou hast said, I am a God, I sit in the seat of God, in the midst of the seas; yet thou art a man, and not God, though thou set thine heart as the heart of God." Then in verse 12 we read "Son of man, take up a lamentation upon the king of Tyrus (prince of Tyrus, verse 2), and say unto him, "Thus saith the Lord God; Thou sealest up the sum, full of wisdom, and perfect in beauty." This isn't addressed to "Satan." Verse 2 states, "thou art a man," whose heart was lifted up and he had said unto himself, "I am God, I sit in the seat of God." Verses 3 and 4 tell us that he was very wise and through his wisdom and understanding he had gotten great wealth. In verses 8-10 we read of his death.

Now, let us read verse 12 again, "Son of man, take up a lamentation upon the king of Tyrus, and say unto him, Thus saith the Lord God; Thou sealest up the sum, full of wisdom and perfect in beauty." We have been taught and have assumed that since it says he was "full of wisdom and perfect in beauty" it must be speaking of "Satan." "Perfect" is used in a relative sense when it isn't speaking of deity, of God. In this passage God is merely shoving this into the king's face, as it was Tyrus who earlier had attributed to herself (the city) this claim of perfect beauty, not God! Notice Ezekiel 27:2-3, "Now, thou son of man, take up a lamentation for Tyrus; And say unto Tyrus, O thou that art situate at the entry of the sea, [which art] a merchant of the people for many isles, Thus saith the Lord God; O Tyrus, thou hast said, I [am] of perfect beauty."

In verse 12 we find an interesting expression, "Thou sealest up..." What does this mean? Notice what some of the commentators tell us.

Commentary accounts

First, from Adam Clarke's commentary of Ezekiel 28:12, "Verse 12. Thou sealest up] This has been translated, 'Thou drawest thy own likeness.' 'Thou formest a portrait of thyself; and hast represented thyself the perfection of wisdom and beauty.' I believe this to be the meaning of the place."

John Wesley's comments, "Thou sealest up - Thou fanciest that fulness of wisdom, and perfection of beauty are in thee." And, from Jameison, Faucett and Brown: "12. Sealest up the sum—literally, 'Thou art the one sealing the sum of perfection.' A thing is sealed when completed (Dan. 9:24). 'The sum' implies the full measure of beauty, from a Hebrew root, 'to measure.' The normal man—one formed after accurate rule."

What God is saying in this passage is that it was the king of Tyrus who ascribed to himself the greatest wisdom and perfection of beauty. It clearly is not God who is saying that this individual is "full of wisdom and perfect in beauty."

Back to Ezekiel 28

Let us continue with verse 13 of Ezekiel 28. "Thou hast been in Eden the garden of God; every precious stone [was] thy covering, the sardius, topaz, and the diamond, the beryl, the onyx, and the jasper, the sapphire, the emerald, and the carbuncle, and gold: the workmanship of thy tabrets and of thy pipes was prepared in thee in the day that thou wast created."

We have been told that this verse is a "proof text" that this is speaking of "Satan." After all, wasn't he in the garden of Eden and wasn't he a created being? Let us understand.

The word translated "Eden" in this verse is the same word or root translated "Eden" about 20 times in the Hebrew Scriptures. It does sometimes reference the "garden" that God planted in the area of the country called Eden. But, it sometimes references other lands near the area of Eden and not "the garden" of Eden. It even refers to the "children of Eden" as in II Kings 19:12. And, we all are aware, are we not, that Adam and Eve had NO CHILDREN while they were yet in the "garden of Eden." Amos 1:5 speaks of the "house of Eden." Again, this is the same Hebrew word translated "Eden" in every occurrence of this word in the Hebrew Manuscripts. And, by the way, Eden is the name of several individuals in Scripture.

So, we see that "Eden" can mean various things, even though Eden is always translated from the same Hebrew word, which is Strong's H5731. Strong's definition is *"Eden,* ay'-den; the same as H5730, *eden,* ay'den, from H5727, pleasure. H5727, *adan,* aw-dan, to be soft or pleasant...to live voluptuously."

This is a word that has meaning, not just a name. And, it is a word that does not need to be capitalized, nor is it capitalized or even translated "eden" in other Scriptures. Let us notice a couple. "Therefore Sarah laughed within herself, saying, After I am old shall I have pleasure [Hebrew translated 'pleasure' here is *eden,* ay-den] my lord being old also?" (Gen. 18:12) "They shall be abundantly satisfied with the fatness of your house; and you shalt make them drink of the river of your pleasures [Hebrew translated 'pleasures' here is *eden,* ay-den']." (Psa. 36:8)

So, I ask, why should it be capitalized in Ezekiel 28:13? The answer is, it shouldn't! Here are a couple of translations which don't capitalize it or even translate it "eden." "Thou wast in the pleasures [Heb. *eden,* ay-den'] of the paradise [or garden] of God." (Ezek. 28:13, The Holy Bible, Douay Confraternity) "In the luxury [Heb. *eden*, ay-den'] of the garden of Alueim [God] you come to be." (Ezek. 28:13, The Concordant Literal Old Testament)

What is this about "every precious stone was thy covering?" Nine stones plus gold are mentioned. If you will remember, there was a very special privileged relationship that Tyre had with Israel. King David of Israel had been a close friend of Hiram, the king of Tyre. In 2 Sam. 5:11 we read of Hiram sending messengers to David along with material and workmen, and they built David a house. Later Solomon made an alliance with Hiram in which Hiram supplied materials for the building of the temple. What we are reading here in Ezekiel is in reference to the Israelites' worship of God and, by implication, suggests that this king of Tyre had divine favor resting on him because of his association with Israel. Consider for a bit the following.

"Every precious stone was thy covering" (verse 13 that we just read); "thou hast walked up and down in the midst of the stones of fire" (verse

14 which we hadn't yet come to). This seems very much to be an allusion to the stones set in the breastplate of the high priest (Ex. 39:10-14; Ex.28:15-21) Ezekiel refers to them as "stones of fire" because of the way they would shine. They symbolized the twelve tribes of Israel. The king of Tyre walked in the midst of these stones of fire when he moved among the children of Israel as they prepared the materials for the temple. The position of Israel in God's divine purpose provided a "covering" for Tyre. We can base this on what we read in Genesis 12:3, as spoken to Abraham, "And I will bless them that bless thee, and curse him that curseth thee:..." We know that God blessed the house of Potiphar in Egypt because of Joseph, "the LORD blessed the Egyptian's house for Joseph's sake; and the blessing of the LORD was upon all that he had in the house, and in the field." (Gen. 39:4) Similarly, Tyre was "covered" by the LORD.

(Note: Although there were twelve stones set in the breastplate in settings of gold the King James Version lists only nine stones here. However, the Septuagint, the Greek translation of the Old Testament lists all twelve here in Ezekiel 28, plus chrysolite and silver.)

Let us move to the end of verse 13, "...in the day that thou wast created." This is speaking of a created being and therefore couldn't it mean "Satan" as opposed to the King of Tyrus who was born rather than created? Not at all!

Whether a person is born of a woman or is created directly out of the dust of the ground as was Adam, they are both "creations of God." We find a number of Scriptures that show that "created" can be applied to those born of a woman. "But now thus says the Lord that created thee, O Jacob, and He that formed you, O Israel..." (Isa. 43:1) "...bring my sons from far, and my daughters from the ends of the earth; Even every one that is called by My name: for I have created him; yea, I have made him" (Isa. 43:6-7) "Thus says the Lord God concerning the Ammonites...I will judge you [Ammonites] in the place where you were created..." (Ezek. 21:28 & 30) "Have we not all one father? Has not one God created US [all mankind]" (Mal. 2:10)

EZEKIEL 28:14

But, what about verse 14? Surely we have no further use of discussing this, surely this is not a human but a cherub. Doesn't this verse clearly prove that this is "Satan" and not some human? No! It actually proves only that we have a very bad translation. Let's look at the verse.

Ezekiel 28:14, "Thou [art] the anointed cherub that covereth; and I have set thee so: thou wast upon the holy mountain of God; thou hast walked up and down in the midst of the stones of fire. (King James Version)

Let's look at a few other translations of this verse.

"On the day you were created, I placed you beside the kherubs on the sacred hill of God; you walked amid the flashing thunder-stones." (Ezek. 28:14 A New Translation by James Moffatt)

"In the day of your creation they established the anointed cherub's booth. And I bestow you in the holy mountain of Alueim [God]." (Ezek. 28:14 Concordant Version of the Old Testament)

"With an anointed cherub as guardian I place you; you were on the holy mountain of God; you walked among the stones of fire." (Ezek. 28:14 The New Revised Standard Version)

"With the Cherub I placed you; you were on the holy mountain of God, walking among the fiery stones." (Ezek. 28:14 The New American Bible)

"I gave you your place with the winged one; I put you on the mountain of God; you went up and down among the stones of fire." (Ezek. 29:14 The Bible in Basic English)

"You were with the anointed cherub that shelters; and I have set you on the holy mountain of God; and you were safe in the midst of the stones of fire." (Ezek. 28:14 Holy Bible From the Ancient Eastern Text, George M. Lamsa's translation from the Aramatic of the Peshita)

Hopefully, two things become clear from reading these various translations: (1) This verse is a challenge to translate, and (2) the prince of Tyre was NOT the cherub but rather the cherub was placed as a guardian with or beside the prince of Tyre.

Granted we do not know a great deal about cherubs or cherubim. From Scripture we know that they are not cute little chubby babies with tiny wings holding bows and arrows but are spirit creatures with great power, and yes, with wings. God placed cherubim at the garden of Eden to guard the way of the tree of life. They were carved and made of gold and placed on the cover of the ark of the covenant. They also were associated with the decorations of the tabernacle and later the temple. And, we find them associated with the throne of God.

We know that God has two groups of spiritual messengers. One group carries out acts of good while the other carries out acts of deceit and wickedness, i.e. evil. Notice I Kings 22:19; "...I saw the LORD sitting on his throne, and all the host of heaven (angelic beings) standing by him on his right hand (the good) and on his left (the evil)." We are reminded of the account in Matthew 25, when Messiah returns He shall gather the nations and separate them as a shepherd divides the sheep and the goats. Those on the right hand are to inherit the kingdom, but those on the left hand are told to depart into the fire. (Matt. 25:31-41)

As mentioned, we find cherubim associated with the Throne of God and the possibility that there are cherubim associated with the throne of world leaders is very plausible. Whatever their earthly function, as guardians, etc., there was a cherub associated with the king of Tyrus. He was with or beside the king. He was not the king. And, there is absolutely no indication that the cherub was the adversary.

What about the statement "thou wast upon the holy mountain of God;"? Doesn't that indicate this individual had been in heaven? No, numerous Scriptures plainly tell us that the mountain of God is Mt. Zion, here on earth. Micah 4:2, "And many nations shall come, and say, Come, and let us go up to the mountain of the LORD, and to the house of the God of Jacob; and he will teach us of his ways, and we will walk in his paths: for the law shall go forth of Zion, and the word of the LORD from Jerusalem." Joel 3:17, "So shall ye know that I am the LORD your God dwelling in Zion, my holy mountain: then shall Jerusalem be holy, and there shall no strangers pass through her any more."

Ezekiel 28:15-19

Let us continue with verse 15 of Ezekiel 28. "Thou [wast] perfect in thy ways from the day that thou wast created, till iniquity was found in thee." We have been taught that this is speaking of a being that was created perfect, in other words a spirit being The Hebrew word translated "perfect" is H8549 in Strong's, *tamiym*. Some of the meanings given are "complete, whole, entire, sound, unimpaired, innocent, having integrity." This man, this ruler, this king, had integrity until iniquity, sin, was found in him. And, what was that sin? Having his heart lifted up and saying that he was a God (verse 2).

Verse 16 continues, "By the multitude of thy merchandise they have filled the midst of thee with violence, and thou hast sinned: therefore I will cast thee as profane out of the mountain of God: and I will destroy thee, O covering cherub, from the midst of the stones of fire."

Let us begin to understand. Notice again verses 4 and 5. This man had "gotten thee riches," verse 4 and "by thy traffick hast thou increased thy riches," verse 5. Exactly what verse 16 is saying, "by the multitude of thy merchandise." "And thou hast sinned," is what we read in verse 15, "till iniquity was found in thee."

But, what about the last part of verse 16? Is it the ruler, the king of Tyrus or the cherub that God says is going to die, to be destroyed? Verses 8-10 seem quite plain that it is the man, the king of Tyrus that is to die but this verse seems to imply that the "covering cherub" is the one to be destroyed, doesn't it? Just as we saw in verse 14 that it was the cherub that was with the king, we have a similar translation difficulty here.

Let us look at a couple of other translations.

First of all from the Revised Standard Version. Ezek. 28:16, "In the abundance of your trade you were filled with violence, and you sinned; so I cast you as a profane thing from the mountain of God, and the guardian cherub drove you out from the midst of the stones of fire."

The Bible in Basic English renders it this way: Ezekiel 28:16, "Through all your trading you have become full of violent ways, and have done evil: so I sent you out shamed from the mountain of God; the winged one put an end to you from among the stones of fire."

The language is poetic but it seems clear that the protection, the guardianship given by the cherub was to be removed. Notice verses 17-19. This man was to be laid before kings and they would behold him (verse 17). He was to be brought to ashes (spirit beings can't be turned into ashes) upon the earth in the sight of all that beheld him (verse 18). Verse 19 says, "All they that know thee among the people," (This isn't a spirit being.) "And never shalt thou be any more." One called "Satan" is still around.

God gave Ezekiel these words (verse 1) regarding the prince or king of Tyrus. The nineteen verses we have just looked at were to and about this individual. Some of the language is poetic. In some areas we find the translation has been difficult. But, when we read it with understanding, we see that it is not talking about a spirit or angelic being but about a man. These nineteen verses are a continuation of the prophecy and lamentation against Tyrus the city, and the prince or king. Chapter 26, as we looked at in the beginning of this study, is totally about Tyrus. We found that chapter 27 is another lamentation for Tyrus, verses 1 and 2. Chapter 28 continues with God's words against this city and this king. Remember, originally there were no chapter breaks. The narrative just continues from chapter 26:1 through chapter 28:19. And, verse 20 continues with Tyre's sister city Sidon or Zidon. There is not anything here in these three chapters about a "perfect angelic being" rebelling against God and becoming "Satan."

CHAPTER THREE

THE SATAN OF THE BIBLE

The Bible does NOT tell us that the one called the devil is named Satan. "What?" you may ask! Although the King James Version and most of the translations we read have the word capitalized and treated as a proper name the Hebrew and Greek DO NOT give any indication of a need for capitalization or any indication of the original being a proper name.

HEBREW AND GREEK

The Hebrew word is *satan*, saw-tawn', H7854 in Strong's. It has the meaning of "adversary, one who withstands". The word is used of human adversaries as well as a spirit adversary. The Hebrew *satan* is used 27 times in the Old Testament, only 19 are translated "Satan." In 2 of those Scriptures the original shows the translation to be "an adversary" and the other 17 to be "the adversary." The article "the" is very definitely used in all of those 17 places. And, the article "the" is NEVER used with a proper name. In the Hebrew it is not proper to say "the Jacob" or "the Moses." The translators have arbitrarily left out the article "the" and capitalized the word "satan" in English.

The New Testament Greek word is *satanas*, sat-an-as', #G4567 in Strong's. This Greek form is derived from the Aramaic and Hebrew word *satan,* an adversary. The meaning in Greek as well as Hebrew is "adversary." All 36 places this word appears, the translators have translated it into English as "satan" and have capitalized it, indicating it is a proper name. 31 of the 36 places the word is translated "satan" the Young's Literal Bible shows the article "the" is in the original. In the other 5 places not having the article "the", it indicates the translation would be more proper as "adversary." Even the Young and the Weymouth translations, which translate most of these as "adversary," have incorrectly capitalized the word, even though there is no grammatical reason to do so in the Greek

As mentioned, the Hebrew word *satan* means "enemy, adversary." It is used in this sense numerous times in the Old Testament to refer to human adversaries or enemies. Let's look at a few examples. "And the Lord stirred up an adversary (Hebrew *satan*) unto Solomon, Hadad the Edomite;..."(1 Kings 11:14) And again, verse 23, "And God stirred him up another adversary (Hebrew *satan*), Rezon the son of Eliadah, which fled from his lord Hadadezer king of Zobah." Verse 25, "And he was an adversary (Hebrew *satan*) to Israel all the days of Solomon... In these 3 verses we see two individuals, Hadad and Rezon, were *satans* of Israel, that is, they were enemies and adversaries of Israel. Did you know that King David was also a *satan*? Notice 1 Samuel 29. In verse 3 we see that David is being talked about, "Is not this David, the servant of Saul the king of Israel..." Then in verse 4, "and let him not go down with us to battle, lest in battle he be an adversary (Hebrew *satan*) to us..." They were concerned that David would turn against them in the middle of battle and become their enemy, their *satan*. So,

King David, the anointed of God, was a *satan* (enemy) to the Philistines. There are quite a number of other Scriptures that you can look at that show the Hebrew *satan* being a human enemy, an adversary. We see that a *satan* is quite simply an enemy, someone who hates and seeks harm. A *satan* is not even necessarily evil since King David was a *satan* to the evil Philistines.

ANGELIC ADVERSARY

We do find many references to an angelic adversary. Contrary to what Christianity has taught us "the adversary" has not been identified by name. All we have from Scripture is a reference to an angelic adversary. The first reference to an angelic *satan* (enemy or adversary) is in the account of the Gentile prophet Balaam. Most of us are familiar with the account in Numbers 22. Balaam had been invited by the Moabite king Balak to curse Israel, but God instructed him not to agree to Balak's request. Balak would not take "no" for an answer, and God eventually agreed that Balaam might go to meet with Balak, but he was not to curse Israel. But, as we know, Balaam had other ideas and set off to curse Israel. God was displeased by this and sent an angelic *satan* against Balaam. Notice Numbers 22:22, "And God's anger was kindled because he went: and the angel of the Lord stood in the way for an adversary (Hebrew *satan*) against him..." We see here the angel of God was a *satan*, an adversary or enemy, to Balaam. In verses 23, 24, 25, 26, 27, 31, 32, 34, and 35 we read that this angelic *satan* is "the angel of the Lord." Notice verse 32, "And the angel of the Lord said unto him, Wherefore hast thou smitten thine ass these three times? behold,

I went out to withstand thee (marginal reading is 'to be an adversary unto thee' and the Hebrew is *satan*), because thy way is perverse before me:"

Most of us have never heard that the "angel of the Lord" was *satan* have we? This angelic *satan* is not out to win over millions in an unholy war against God. He is God's angel. The Hebrew word for angel is *mal'ach*, which means "messenger." The representatives sent by Balak to Balaam are also called *mal'achim*, messengers (Num. 22:5). The angelic *satan* in the account of Balaam is simply God's messenger who does what God sends him to do.

It is also clear from the fact that he speaks the message of God both as himself, and as if he were God. Numbers 22:35, "And the angel of Lord said unto Balaam, Go with the men: but only the word that I shall speak unto thee, that thou shalt speak..." This angelic *satan* refers to the words that God will speak to Balaam as "the word that I shall speak unto thee." This is because he is speaking the words God told him to speak, which is the role of a messenger. Balak's messengers did the same thing. In verse 5 they refer to Israel as a people that "abide over against me," the "me" being Balak. They spoke the words of Balak in the first person as if Balak was speaking, in the same way the angelic *satan* speaks the words of God in the first person as if God were saying them. It was the practice of the ancient messengers to freely switch off between speaking their message as if they were the sender and speaking it as themselves.

The angelic *satan* that was sent to harm Balaam did not desire for Balaam to sin. He was not a tempter. He actually ordered Balaam not to defy God. He was simply a messenger of God, and like human messengers, he could speak the words of God in the first person as if he were God. Clearly this angelic *satan* was not a rebellious angel seeking to establish a kingdom of evil. We see that an angel that is sent to cause harm to human beings can be referred to as a *satan* (an adversary, an enemy). The angelic *satan* was not an enemy of God, but His messenger. An enemy or adversary causes harm so an angel that causes harm to human beings can be called a *satan*.

Let's look at another angelic *satan*, the account being found in the book of Zechariah. The prophet Zechariah sees two angels standing near the high priest, "And he shewed me Joshua the high priest standing before the angel of the Lord, and Satan (the *satan*, the adversary) standing at his right hand to resist (to be a *satan*) to him." (Zech. 3:1) The vision continues, "And the Lord said unto Satan (the *satan*, the adversary, the enemy), The Lord rebuke thee, O Satan (*satan*, enemy, adversary); even the Lord that hath chosen Jerusalem rebuke thee: is not this a brand plucked out of the fire?" (Zech. 3:2) We see in this vision that the angelic *satan* wants to harm Joshua the high priest but God calls him off because it would cause harm to Jerusalem. Joshua here is likened to a brand saved from the fire, that is, a stick of wood about to be burned up that is plucked from the bonfire. Joshua was supposed to be burned up by God's wrath, but God gave him a last minute reprieve, not for his own sake but for the sake of Jerusalem. After he is saved from his punishment we read that Joshua's soiled clothes are removed and he is dressed in fine robes (verses 3-5). The dirty clothes symbolized being covered in sin and worthy of punishment. The angelic *satan* had been sent to punish Joshua. God forgave Joshua and canceled the punishment; he called off the angelic *satan*. The angelic *satan* in this account, like in the account of Balaam, was sent to punish when God's wrath was burning ("a brand plucked from the fire") and in both cases the mission to harm is canceled at the last minute.

We read that God rebuked the angel. Let us understand. There is one other scripture that speaks about an angelic *satan* on someone's right hand. In Psalms 109:6 King David asks God to punish those who have harmed him, "Set thou a wicked man over him: and let Satan (Hebrew a *satan*) stand at his right hand." King David is praying that his enemies be punished by God, "appointing" an evil human to rule over them or an angelic *satan* who will harm them. The angelic *satan* who comes to the right hand to do harm is "appointed" by God. We should not be surprised to see that God rebukes the very angelic *satan* He Himself appointed to harm Joshua the high priest. The ability to rescind His own decree of punishment is said to be one of the merciful traits of God. "But he, being full of compassion, forgave their iniquity, and destroyed them not: yea, many a time turned he his anger away, and did not stir up all his wrath." (Psa. 78:38)

God can "turn back His anger" and forgive, canceling the punishment that He has already decreed. We know He did this for the Israelites after they worshiped the golden calf. (Psa. 106:23) He also did this for Joshua the high priest. Joshua's soiled clothes, picturing being covered in sin and worthy of punishment, are removed, and he is dressed in fine robes (Zech 3:4). When God rebukes the angelic *satan* this is an act of "turning back His anger." The angelic *satan* was "appointed" on Joshua's "right hand" to punish him for his sins. God decided to forgive Joshua and canceled the punishment and removed his sin. He recalled the angelic *satan* He had sent to execute His wrath.

Not the "Satan" of Christianity

In the examples we have looked at, we have seen no indication of a "Christian concept of Satan." There are, however, a number of instances in the Hebrew Scriptures in which an angelic *satan* does seek to lead men to sin. Let's look at some of them and see if we see the Satan pictured most often by Christianity.

Let us look at the account of the census of King David. The Torah required that each person participating in a census pay a half shekel of silver to the Temple as "a ransom (an atonement) for his soul unto the Lord, when thou numberest them; that there be no plague among them, when thou numberest them." (Exodus 30:12) This was done by writing down the names of all who paid the half shekel and then counting the names on the list (Ex. 30:13; Num. 1:2). To simply send around a census-taker to count the people was a grievous sin that would bring God's wrath on the nation. This is where the angelic *satan* enters the story. "And Satan (the *satan*, the adversary, the enemy) stood up against Israel, and provoked David to number Israel." (1 Chron. 21:1)

David, as we know from the story, gave in to the *satan's* incitement or provocation and he counted Israel which resulted in a devastating plague that killed thousands.

David's census is also mentioned in a parallel account in the book of 2 Samuel. We know that many of the accounts in the books of Samuel and Kings are repeated in the books of Chronicles, sometimes verbatim, other times with additional information. In the case of David's census we find some additional information. Let's notice 2 Samuel 24:1. "And again the anger of the Lord was kindled against Israel, and he moved David against them to say, Go, number Israel and Judah." Here we see that the one who incited, provoked, David was God! We just read in 2 Samuel that it was a *satan*. We saw in the Balaam account that angelic *satans* are messengers of God who do His bidding, even speaking His words in the first person, like human messengers or prophets. So when we read in one book that God incited Israel and in the other that a *satan* was the one doing the inciting, we must conclude that this *satan* was acting on God's behalf. It is not unusual at all to attribute the actions of the messenger to the one who sent him. The sender is credited with the actions of the messenger acting on his behalf. The angelic *satan* provoked David on God's behalf, so it can be said that God provoked David. Chronicles informs us that He did it by sending an angelic *satan*.

I believe it is worth noting that David was not tempted by the angelic *satan*, but was incited or provoked. To incite in the Hebrew means to urge or otherwise influence someone to do something wrong.

For example, "If thy brother...entice (incite) thee secretly, saying, Let us go and serve other gods" (Deut. 13:6) We can only guess how the angelic *satan* urged David to count the people. From Joab's reaction (2 Sam. 24:3; 2 Chron. 21:3) it seems that David may have suffered from a sense of inferiority and desired to know how many people he ruled over so he could feel mighty. Possibly the angelic *satan* even planted this seed of inferiority within David at God's behest. David COULD HAVE controlled his desire to sin, but he chose to satisfy himself rather than obey God's commandment.

Why did God incite David to sin? The book of Samuel tells us, "And again the anger of the Lord was kindled against Israel, and he moved David against them..." (2 Sam. 24:1) God was angry at Israel so He sent an angelic *satan* to incite David to sin. We will recall that the angelic *satan* was also sent against Balaam because God was angry with him. When God was angry he often sent angelic *satans* to punish mankind. Balaam was nearly punished by being struck down by the angel. When God was angry at Israel, rather than immediately striking them down, He incited David to cause them to further sin and thereby receive greater punishment. This also gave them an opportunity to resist sinning and to receive forgiveness. This is exactly what God explained to Cain back in the book of Genesis. "If thou doest well, shalt thou not be accepted (forgiveness)? and if thou doest not well (do not do good, do what is right), sin lieth at the door (pictured as an animal or a beast, i.e. the angelic *satan*). And unto thee shall be his desire (he will tempt you to further sin), and thou shalt rule over him (BUT you can resist and not sin). This calls to mind the New Testament Scripture, "Resist the devil, and he will flee from you." (James 4:7)

THE ACCOUNT OF JOB

The most detailed account of the angelic *satan* in the Hebrew Scriptures is found in the book of Job. In the first two chapters of the book we read about two encounters between God and the angelic *satan*, the enemy or the adversary. The fact that this angel is called "the *satan*," the enemy or the adversary, proves that "Satan" was not his name. In Biblical Hebrew a proper noun (i.e. a name) cannot be preceded by the word "the." In Hebrew it is impossible to say "the David" or "the Jacob." The angel in Job is called "the *satan*," which tells us that *satan* is a description of the angel, not his name. The angel in Job is "the enemy," that is, the enemy that was sent to harm Job.

"Now there was a day when the sons of God (angels) came to present themselves before the Lord, and Satan (Hebrew the *satan*, the adversary) came also among them." (Job 1:6) God is described much as a king holding a royal court. Instead of royal courtiers and officials, the heavenly court is attended by the "sons of God," the angels, including the angelic *satan* that would be sent against Job. The account continues with an exchange between God and the angelic *satan*. God declares that Job is the most righteous man on earth and the angelic *satan* responds that this is only because God has protected him. "But," suggests the angel, "put forth thine hand now, and touch all that he hath, and he will curse thee to thy face." (Job 1:11) God agrees to the *satan's* suggestion and instructs the angelic *satan*, "Behold, all that he hath is in thy power; only upon himself put not forth thine hand." (Verse 12) The angelic *satan* is given permission to destroy all that Job has but not to touch Job himself. We see that this angelic *satan* proceeds to kill Job's children and destroy his property. The angel is called a *satan* because he is an enemy who harms Job.

In Job chapter two we read of a second encounter between God and this angelic *satan*. This time the angelic *satan* suggests that God harm Job's body, "But put forth thine hand now, and touch his bone and his flesh, and he will curse thee to thy face." (Job 2:5) How does God respond? He grants the angelic *satan* permission to harm Job's person, "Behold, he is in thine hand; but save his life." (Verse 6) What we see is God smiting Job by giving him over into the hands of his angelic *satanic* messenger.

Just to what extent is this angelic *satan* an independent creature? Notice, he can only do what God allows him to do. While Job was under God's protection the angelic *satan* was powerless to do anything to him. The angel complained to God, "Hast not thou made an hedge about him, and about his house, and about all that he hath on every side?" (Job 1:10) When God was ready to test Job He removed His protection and turned him over to the angelic *satan,* just as He did to Balaam and David. Yet the actions of this angelic *satan* are said to be God's actions. Remember we read in chapter one, verse 11, where the angel suggests to God, "But put forth thine hand now, and touch all that he hath,..." God puts forth His hand against Job and his property by giving it over to this angelic *satan*.

We find once again that the sender is given credit for the actions of the messenger. Like the "sin beast" in the Cain account lying at the door, Job's angelic *satan* lay waiting for Job to sin. This angelic *satan's* mission from God was not simply to punish a man or mankind, but to try and get him to sin so the man or mankind could receive an even greater punishment. The angelic *satan* DID NOT do this on his own account or initiative. He was sent by God to wander to and fro in the earth and to tempt those who have sinned to sin further or to test those whom God wished to test.

CONCLUSIONS FROM THE OLD TESTAMENT

From the Old Testament Scriptures we have seen several things. "Satan" is not a fallen archangel named Lucifer. (See Chapter One, "Lucifer is not Satan!".) Angelic *satans* aren't enemies of mankind. They are simply messengers who do God's bidding. Some fulfill the role of a "sin beast" that crouches or lies at the door, waiting to pounce on the sinner. The angelic *satan* in Chronicles fulfilled this role and was sent by God to incite David to sin. In Job the angelic *satan* was at first helpless to cause Job to sin, because God protected Job (Job 1:10). But when God wanted to test Job He did this by allowing the angelic *satan* to tempt him. Despite the horrible things that happened to Job, we find that he succeeded in ruling over the great temptation to sin. Although he was turned over into the hands of the angelic *satan*, Job was able, by acting righteously, to rule over the angelic *satan* rather than be ruled by it.

What about the New Testament?

But, surely, when we come to the New Testament we will find a great personage named "Satan" who wars against God and mankind, right? Wrong! What we find is a continuation of what we found in the Old Testament. The Greek word *satanas* directly corresponds to the Hebrew *satan* and means the same thing, "adversary (one who opposes another in purposes or act)". Every place this word, *satanas*, Strong's G4567, is used it is translated in the King James Version as "Satan," with the word being capitalized, although grammatically there is no reason for it. 31 times out of the 36 the word is used, the Greek shows the definite article "the" is in the original, the *satanas*, the adversary.

The other 5 times *satanas* is used the word would properly be translated as "adversary" or "enemy." Let us take a quick look at those 5 passages. "Then saith Jesus unto him, Get thee hence, *satanas* (adversary), for it is written," (Matt. 4:10) In the context here we see Jesus is going through His great temptation by "the devil," verse 1. Verse 2 calls him "the tempter." Neither "devil" or "tempter" is a name but a description. Devil is from the Greek *diabolos*, Strong's G1228, meaning slanderer, accuser. Tempter is from the Greek *peirazo*, Strong's G3985, meaning to try, make trial or test. These two words are, as I said, descriptions and so is the word *satanas,* adversary. The angelic *satanas* is also an angelic *diabolos* and an angelic *peirazo*. Jesus describes him as adversary, slanderer and tempter. A second passage is found in Luke 4:8. It is a parallel Scripture to this one in Matthew.

The third and fourth passages are parallel accounts. Let us notice Matthew 16:23, "But he turned, and said unto Peter, Get thee behind me *satanas* (adversary): thou art an offence unto me: for thou savourest not the things that be of God, but those that be of men." The parallel account is in Mark 8:33. Jesus is addressing Peter. He doesn't call him "Satan" as a name. He calls him an adversary. Peter was an adversary or an enemy to Jesus at that time. (See Chapter Four.)

The fifth passage is located in the book of Revelation, chapter 20 and verse 2. "And he laid hold on the dragon, that old serpent, which is the *diabolos*, and *satanas*, and bound him a thousand years." Here we see descriptions, not names. Dragon, serpent, slanderer, adversary are descriptions of this angelic messenger from God. These are all descriptions of the activities this angelic being has been given to do by God.

There is one other term or word that we read frequently in the New Testament, devils or demons. There are 3 different Greek words, 2 being derivatives of the other one. G1142 in Strong's is *daimon*, which means simply an evil spirit. G1140 is derived from G1142 and is *daimonion* and is the most frequently used of the three. It again means evil spirits. The third word, used in reference to being possessed by an evil spirit is, G1139, *daimonizomai*. From Revelation 12:4 we do get an indication that about one third of the angels are "evil spirits," and are referred to as the dragon's angels, verses 7 and 9.

WHERE DID THE ADVERSARY COME FROM?

If the one referred to as the adversary isn't a fallen archangel, once named Lucifer, just where did he come from? I think we have clearly shown that the one called the adversary is an angel that was created by God. But, surely He didn't create an "evil spirit?" Yes, most definitely He did. We try to reason around the scripture over in Isaiah 45:7, "I form the light (which we can agree with), and create darkness (okay with that): I make peace (yes, God is the Peacemaker), and create evil (What?): I the Lord do all these things." Yes, God says he created evil (Strong's number H7451). Interestingly enough, among the many definitions for this Hebrew word *rah* or *ra'ah* is "adversity." The adversary, the one bringing adversity, was created by God. Notice a very clear Scripture in which God tells us plainly that He created him, Job 26:13. "By his spirit he hath garnished the heavens; his hand hath formed the crooked serpent." Revelation 20:2 tells us plainly "that old serpent, which is the Devil, and Satan,..." We know that it was the adversary in the form of a serpent that appeared to Eve in the garden.

God is sovereign. He is omnipotent, omniscient and omnipresent. He is able to do all; He knows all; He is present everywhere at the same time. He is the producer of all. Look at Romans 11:36, "For of him, and through him, and to him, are all things: to whom be glory for ever. Amen."

God is able to do all. He is quite able to keep the adversary from going contrary to His intentions and He is able to have him do whatever is in accord with His intentions and plan. God knows all, even the end from the beginning (Isa. 46:10) and the adversary has never deceived Him. God knew beforehand just what the adversary was going to do at all times. God being present everywhere at the same time, the adversary has never been able to hide from God. Since God made ALL things He is the creator and maker of the adversary. God's plans are not being thwarted by this angelic being. Instead God uses him to carry out His plan. God brought the adversary into being, for all is out of God (Rom. 11:36), and God determined beforehand that sin would enter the universe through the acts of the adversary. We must understand that it is God who is doing all things according to His purpose and will. "...according to the purpose of him who worketh all things (this includes the adversary) after the counsel of his own will." (Eph. 1:11)

This adversary has been given great power and authority. The only one having greater power and authority is the Messiah, who prepared for the trial from the adversary by fasting for forty days and nights. Many believe that the adversary has one third of the angels assisting him in his job. (Rev. 12:4) If so, this also is according to the will of God.

The adversary was on hand at the time of the creation of mankind. God's purpose for mankind included a need for adversity, a need for the tempter, a need for the deceiver, a need for the slanderer. Do I understand just exactly why? NO, not totally. But, much is revealed within the Job account. The testing and trials brought upon Job, as terrible and evil as they were, served God's great purpose. Each of us must be tried and tested, must be purified through fire. God is using the adversary to blind mankind until such time as God desires to open each ones mind to truth. (2 Cor. 4:4; Matt. 13:15) He uses the adversary to deceive all of us, for His purpose

The adversary of mankind was on the scene from the beginning. We find him referred to as a serpent in the garden tempting mother Eve. He was there when Cain rose up and killed Abel. Jesus reveals a bit about the adversary, recorded in John 8:44. "Ye are of your father the devil, and the lusts of your father ye do. He was a murderer from the beginning, and abode not in the truth, because there is no truth in him. When he speaketh a lie, he speaketh of his own: for he is a liar, and the father of it." God cannot lie (Titus 1:2) but He has created this adversary to whom He has given a job that involves lying, slandering and inciting to sins of all types. God is responsible. It is His plan and purpose that the adversary be here. There is not some great fallen archangel and a bunch of rebellious angels that are thwarting God's plan. The adversary and his angels are doing what God instructs them to do and no more. These messengers of God never operate beyond the parameters set by God.

Note: We will look at the adversary's origin further in chapter 7

CHAPTER FOUR

"GET THEE BEHIND ME, SATAN"

DID JESUS CALL PETER "SATAN?"

We read in Matthew 16:23 and in the parallel account in Mark 8:33 that Jesus said to Peter, "Get thee behind me, Satan: thou art an offence unto me: for thou savourest not the things that be of God, but those that be of men." Was the Messiah calling Peter "Satan" or the devil? No! Not at all. Let us understand just what is going on here.

The Greek word translated "Satan" is *satanas* and directly corresponds to the Hebrew *satan* and means the same thing, adversary. That is, "one who opposes another in purposes or act." Every place that this word, *satanas*, Strong's G4567, is used, it is translated in the King James Version as "Satan," with the word being capitalized, although grammatically there is no reason for it. 31 times out of the 36 the word is used, the Greek shows the definite article "the" is in the original, the *satanas*, the adversary.

The other 5 times *satanas* is used, the word would properly be translated as "adversary" or "enemy." Let us take a quick look at those 5 passages. "Then saith Jesus unto him, Get thee hence, *satanas* (adversary), for it is written," (Matt. 4:10). In the context here, we see Jesus is going through His great temptation by "the devil," verse 1. Verse 2 calls him "the tempter." Neither "devil" nor "tempter" is a name but a description. Devil is from the Greek *diabolos*, Strong's G1228, meaning "slanderer, accuser". Tempter is from the Greek *peirazo*, Strong's G3984, meaning "to try, make trial or test". These two words are, as I said, descriptions and so is the word *satanas*, adversary. The angelic *satanas* is also an angelic *diabolos* and an angelic *peirazo*. Jesus describes him as adversary, slanderer and tempter. A second passage in Luke 4:8 is a parallel scripture to this one in Matthew.

The third and fourth passages are the ones we referenced in the opening paragraph, and which we will come back to in a moment. Let us look at the 5th passage, Revelation 20:2. "And he laid hold on the dragon, that old serpent, which is the Devil, and Satan, and bound him a thousand years." The dragon, serpent, *diablos* (devil) and *satanas* (satan) are all descriptions; none of these are names.

Now back to Matthew 16:23. As we read, Jesus is addressing Peter. Let us read it as it should be translated. "...Get thee behind me, adversary:" He doesn't call him "Satan" as a name. He calls him an adversary, one who is opposing Him in what He had to do. At that moment Peter was an adversary or an enemy to Jesus.

COMMENTARIES

This is just an unfortunate translation and one that has been perpetuated by most translators, yet it is common knowledge. Here are just a couple of quotations from some common Bible commentators.

From Adam Clarke's commentary of Matthew 16:23. "Get thee behind me, Satan - (he gives the Greek which I won't put in) Get behind me, thou adversary. This is the proper translation of the Hebrew word *satan*, from which the Greek word is taken. Our blessed Lord certainly never designed that men should believe he called Peter, Devil..."

Quoting from Albert Barnes' Notes on the Bible, Matthew 16:23, "Get thee behind me, Satan - The word 'Satan' literally means 'an adversary,' or one who opposes us in the accomplishment of our designs. It applies to the devil commonly, as the opposer or adversary of man; but there is no evidence that the Lord Jesus meant to apply this term to Peter, as signifying that he was Satan or the devil, or that he used the term in anger. He may have used it in the general sense which the word bore as an adversary or opposer; and the meaning may be, that such sentiments as Peter expressed then were opposed to him and his plans...."

Again, the Messiah did not call the disciple Peter a dirty name, did not insinuate that Peter was the great adversary or was possessed or influenced by that being. He called him what he was at that moment, an adversary, one that was opposing what He, the Messiah, had to do and face.

CHAPTER FIVE

LUKE 10:18 I BEHELD SATAN...

You will remember a quotation I shared in the Introduction.[7] "Tertullian (160-220) was the first of the church fathers who taught that Satan was a fallen angel, by quoting Ezekiel 28 (Against Marcion 2:10). Origen (c.185-c.254) also quoted Isaiah 14, Ezekiel 28 and Luke 10:18 to teach that Satan, or Lucifer, had fallen from glory in heaven (De Principis 1:5:5, Against Celsus 6:44). Although rejected by the Reformers, this teaching was popularized through Milton's vivid description of Satan's rebellion and fall in Book I of 'Paradise Lost', and now, at least on a popular level in the church, seems to be accepted without being questioned." We have looked at Isaiah 14 and Ezekiel 28 in previous chapters. In this chapter we will look at Luke 10:18 briefly.

LUKE 10

This verse from the King James Version of the Bible says, "And he said unto them, I beheld Satan as lightning fall from heaven." As stated in the above quotation, Origen used this passage, along with the Isaiah and Ezekiel Scriptures we have studied, to teach that the one referred to as Satan or Lucifer had rebelled against God and had been cast out

---

[7] Julian Spriggs https://www.julianspriggs.co.uk/pages/FallOfSatan

of heaven as a result. If one checks the various Bible commentators he will find that quite a number of them will parrot what was taught by Origen and what is believed by most Christians today. However, there are a few who do follow one of the basic rules of Bible study, checking the context of this passage rather than assuming it in some way is linked to the passages in Isaiah and Ezekiel.

Let us go back to verse 1 of this chapter, Luke 10. Here we are told that Jesus appointed 70 others, others being in addition to the 12 apostles He had sent earlier, and sent them out two by two, or in pairs. They were being sent into the very cities and places that Jesus was planning to visit later. What were they being sent to do? After telling them that the harvest truly was great and that He was sending them "forth as lambs among wolves," (verses 2 and 3) He gives them specific instructions. (verses 4-8) Then when we come to verse 9 we read the command He gave them, "And heal the sick that are therein, and say unto them, The kingdom of God is come nigh unto you." He follows this up with more specific instructions. (Verses 10-16)

We aren't told how long they were gone on this mission, but in verse 17 we are told that the 70 returned with joy. They were excited and began sharing with Jesus how the very devils (in the King James Version) or demons, were subject to or obedient unto them through His name, the name of Jesus. Now we come to the verse in question. This is still in the context we have been looking at. Jesus speaks to them in direct reference to their comments about what had happened as they went into these cities. He says that He beheld or saw what was happening, obviously in the spirit. He says He saw the adversary, specifically the evil spirits, immediately depart as quick as lightning, when they commanded them to depart and come out of those they were possessing. In other words He was telling them that at their command in His name the spirits immediately left, as quick as a flash of lightning.

I read through numerous commentaries of this verse. Most tried to connect it with the misunderstood story of Lucifer. Albert Barnes' Notes on the Bible captures the true meaning, I believe. "**I beheld Satan...** - Satan here denotes evidently the prince of the devils who had been cast out by the seventy disciples, for the discourse was respecting their power over evil spirits. Lightning is an image of rapidity or quickness. I saw Satan fall quickly or rapidly – as quick as lightning. The phrase from heaven is to be referred to the lightning, and does not mean that he saw Satan fall from heaven, but that he fell as quick as lightning from heaven or from the clouds. The whole expression then may mean, I saw at your command devils immediately depart, as quick as the flash of lightning. I gave you this power – I saw it put forth – and I give also now, in addition to this, the power to tread on serpents, etc."

Mr. Barnes has identified the heaven being spoken about, the one in which there are clouds that produce lightning. The Bible speaks of three heavens. The first was referred to in Genesis 1:6 as the "firmament," or earth's atmosphere. The second heaven was where the sun and moon were. (Genesis 1:17) The area of God's throne is called the "third heaven." (2 Cor. 12:2) The adversary and the evil spirits were cast out of individuals just as fast as lightning from the clouds.

He is stating that He had given them this power, and He continues with the next verse, verse 19, "Behold, I give unto you power to tread on serpents and scorpions, and over all the power of the enemy: and nothing shall by any means hurt you." Treading on serpents and scorpions appears to be a metaphor for the evil spirits. Following this He continues with verse 20 and tells them that rather than rejoicing because the spirits were subject unto them, "but rather rejoice, because your names are written in heaven."

Luke 10:18 is not in any way speaking of some archangel's rebellion and being cast out of heaven. How often do we confuse an issue by taking what is being taught completely out of context and try to twist the passage into saying something that just isn't there. One is reminded of Peter's statement in 2 Peter 3:16. He states that some of Paul's letters contained things hard to be understood. He continues, "which they that are unlearned and unstable wrest, as they do also the other scriptures, unto their own destruction." "To wrest" means to twist or pervert.

CHAPTER SIX

THE ANGELS THAT SINNED

A disturbing verse for many is found in the second chapter of 2 Peter, verse 4, "For if God spared not the angels that sinned, but cast them down to hell, and delivered them into chains of darkness, to be delivered unto judgement." I was always taught, and I find it is the teaching of the majority of Christian groups and churches, that this verse is speaking of "fallen angels", or demons. But is it? Most often we don't question the teachings of the majority. We assume the teaching to be correct. I believe it behooves us to read this verse in context, to put the whole chapter together, and see exactly what the Apostle Peter was saying.

2 Peter

Let us begin with verse one, "But there were false prophets also among the people, even as there shall be false teachers among you, who privily shall bring in damnable heresies, even denying the Lord that bought them, and bring upon themselves swift destruction." Notice, Peter is telling us that there were, in times past, people who were false prophets. False prophets were and are those who give predictions that are incorrect, that do not come to pass. These individuals were among the people in times past JUST AS there were to be false teachers among us. False teachers, just like false prophets, will be teaching and predicting things that are not true, damnable heresies, Peter says. He says they will even deny the Messiah and will "bring on themselves swift destruction."

Continuing with verse 2 Peter says, "And many shall follow their pernicious ways; by reason of whom the way of truth shall be evil spoken of." Many, he says, will be taken in by those false teachers and will follow their "pernicious ways," the way that leads to destruction. Keep in mind that Peter is still speaking of people; false prophets, false teachers and the many who follow them. Let us go on to verse 3, "And through covetousness shall they with feigned words make merchandise of you: whose judgement now of a long time lingereth not, and their damnation slumbereth not." Peter tells us, as so commonly is the case, these false teachers try to make money and realize financial gain from those they are teaching and instructing. Adam Clarke defines "feigned words" as "counterfeit tales, false narration, pretended facts, lying miracles, fabulous legends." What they are saying is pleasant to listen to, sounds plausible but is in truth lies. Due to this they have brought themselves under the judgment and damnation of God, a time of correction.

Now we come to verse 4, "For if God spared not the angels that sinned, but cast them down to hell, and delivered them into chains of darkness, to be reserved unto judgement;" As stated above, I was always taught that this is referring to "fallen angels" but is it? Does Peter jump from speaking of men, false prophets and false teachers, to talk of "fallen angels?" Well, it says "angels" doesn't it and wasn't it the "fallen angels" that sinned? The Greek word translated into the English word "angels" is G32 in Strong's, *aggelos* or *angelos*. Although it is translated generally "angel" the primary definition and the valid translation used in several places is "a messenger, envoy, one who is sent." Young's Literal Bible translates this word in this very verse "messengers." Let us read it thus and see if the rest of the verse makes sense. "For if God spared not the messengers (those who were sent) that sinned (transgressed God's law), but cast them down to hell and delivered them into chains of darkness," Uh-oh! What have we here? The word translated "hell" in this verse is a Greek word found nowhere else in the entirety of the Bible. It is G5020 in Strong's, *tartaroo*, from *tartaros*.

Tartaroo

What does this word mean? Almost all of the scholars tell us that since it is found only this one time in the Bible we have to look elsewhere. Where we find it used is in Greek mythology. The Greeks believed Tartarus to be the "place of punishment in the lower world." I do not believe, nor do I think most Christians would believe, that Peter is endorsing the nonsense of pagan mythology. If he did, then we would have to accept all of the absurdities that goes along with it. However, many have accepted this teaching, not knowing where it came from. We do know that it is never taught or referred to in the Old Testament or in the New Testament.

Peter does allude to the subject as though it was well-known and understood by his readers. Where is the story of individuals being cast down to Tartaros recorded? As stated above, it isn't in the Scriptures.

However, there was such a story in a book that was well known at the time of his writing, the Book of Enoch. It is from this apocryphal book that Peter seems to refer. By doing so did he sanction it as true, or did he as many writers do, use it to illustrate and enforce his statements regarding the disobedient, the unrighteous, the false prophets being kept for later judgment? I believe it is nothing more than some writers might refer to the story of "the tortoise and the hare." They don't actually believe the story of a race between the two but use the Aesop fable to illustrate or make a point.

Though the account in the Book of Enoch does deal with sinning angels, which the Bible doesn't discuss at all, it seems from the context of this entire chapter (as we will see even clearer as we go on) it is men that Peter is talking about. One writer makes the following comment, "Tartaros—this word occurs only once, in 2 Peter 2:4. A little Bible investigation will reveal that the angels or messengers, God's servants who rebelled, were Korah, Dathan and Abiram–Numbers 16:30-33. The earth opened and swallowed them up. The pit in verses 30 and 33 is Sheol in Hebrew - the GRAVE - and it is there that they await judgment." I haven't studied this enough to be able to say that he is correct but I do believe it is plausible. It certainly makes more sense to me than to believe Peter is speaking of "fallen angels."

Context

If we don't make the assumption that most make, that Peter is speaking of fallen angels, and continue to read in context, we can understand what he is saying. He is stating that these individuals are cast away from God's presence, literally into the earth if it does happen to be Korah, Dathan and Abiram he is referring to. He says that they were delivered "unto chains of darkness." There was literal darkness in that pit but Strong's tells us that darkness is used metaphorically "of ignorance respecting divine things and human duties, and the accompanying ungodliness and immorality." A second definition states, "persons in whom darkness becomes visible and holds sway." God and His truth is Light. The opposite is darkness.

"Chains," as we read here, are not literal. It is rather an indication that these individuals are bound by this darkness, this blindness if you will, until, as the last part of the verse states, the time of judgment. They are "reserved," kept for the purpose of judgment, a time of correction. Many assume judgment is a time of destruction. God's judgment is to correct, with punishment as needed, to bring one to reconciliation.

Let us continue through this chapter and we will see even clearer that Peter has not jumped from his discussion of individual people (false prophets, etc.) to spirit beings. Verse 5, "And spared not the old world, but saved Noah the eighth person, a preacher of righteousness, bringing in the flood upon the world of the ungodly;" Did you notice the same phrase used in verse 4, "And spared not?" Peter is still speaking of people, the old world and speaks of Noah who was righteous. He is contrasted to the ungodly, those outside of the "light" and in the "darkness."

VERSES 6-9

And, in verse 6 Peter continues speaking of people who lived and acted contrary to God and His way of life. "And turning the cities of Sodom and Gomorrha into ashes condemned them with an overthrow, making them an ensample unto those that after should live ungodly;" Peter continues in verse 7 to talk about people. "And delivered just Lot, vexed with the filthy conversation of the wicked;" The contrast continues to be between the righteous, the just, and the ungodly, those in darkness. Continuing to speak of Lot in verse 8 Peter says, "(For that righteous man dwelling among them, in seeing and hearing, vexed his righteous soul from day to day with their unlawful deeds;)" His contrast between the righteous and the unrighteous continues. Verse 9, "The Lord knoweth how to deliver the godly out of temptations and to reserve the unjust unto the day of judgement to be punished;" Did you notice the wording in this verse, "to reserve... unto the day of judgement," is almost identical to what we read in verse 4, "reserved unto judgement." Verse 9 is definitely speaking of people, as the context is making very clear, so also is verse 4.

VERSES 10-13

Let us continue reading with verse 10, "But chiefly them that walk after the flesh (not spirit) in the lust of uncleanness, and despise government. Presumptuous are they, self-willed, they are not afraid to speak evil of dignitaries." Peter is still talking about people, the ungodly, the unrighteous. Verse 11 says, "Whereas angels, which are greater in power and might, bring not railing accusation against them before the

Lord." Does Peter begin speaking of spirit beings, angels? Again the word is *angelos*, which can be just as properly translated "messengers." What "messengers" are greater in "power and might" than the ungodly, the unrighteous? Obviously those that are obeying and following God. In verse 12 it is quite plain that Peter is still speaking of people. "But these, as natural brute beasts, made to be taken and destroyed, speak evil of the things that they understand not; and shall utterly perish in their own corruption;" He says "these" still speaking of the ungodly and amplifying verse 11. He then refers to them as "natural brute beasts," akin to calling them nothing but animals.

Continuing with verse 13, "And shall receive the reward of unrighteousness, as they that count it pleasure to riot in the day time. Spots they are and blemishes, sporting themselves with their own deceivings while they feast with you;" Peter is still speaking of the false teachers, the ungodly. Verse 14 through 16, "Having eyes full of adultery, and that cannot cease from sin; beguiling unstable souls: an heart they have exercised with covetous practices; cursed children; Which have forsaken the right way, and are gone astray, following the way of Balaam the son of Bosor, who loved the wages of unrighteousness; But was rebuked for his iniquity; the dumb ass speaking with man's voice forbad the madness of the prophet." Peter hasn't varied from his theme. He is still talking of the ungodly, the unrighteous, the false prophets, the false teachers.

Verses 17-22

In verse 17 Peter starts out by saying, "These..." just as he began verse 12. The same "these." Let us go on, "These are wells without water, clouds that are carried with a tempest; to whom the mist of darkness is reserved for ever." In verse 12 he said "these, as natural brute beasts," Here he says, "These are wells without water," In both verses he is still speaking of men. Going back to verse 4 we read, "and delivered them into chains of darkness, to be reserved unto judgement." The wording here in verse 17 is similar, "to whom the mist of darkness is reserved for ever." But, doesn't "for ever" indicate for all eternity? No! The Greek is *aion* which is best translated age or ages. Peter is saying that these individuals have been "reserved," kept, in a state of spiritual darkness for the age, until the age or time of judgment.

Peter keeps speaking of these individuals. Verse 18, "For when they speak great swelling words of vanity, they allure through the lusts of the flesh, through much wantonness, those that were clean escaped from them who live in error." Verse 19, "While they promise them liberty, they themselves are the servants of corruption; for of whom a man is overcome, of the same is he brought to bondage." He keeps right on speaking of these individuals that he first called false prophets and false teachers. Verse 20, "For if after they have escaped the pollutions of the world through the knowledge of the Lord and Saviour Jesus they are again entangled therein, and overcome, the latter end is worse with them than the beginning." He is still speaking of people. Verse 21 and 22, "For it had been better for them not to have known the way of righteousness, than, after they have known it, to turn from the holy commandment delivered unto them. But it is happened unto them according to the true proverb, The dog is turned to his own vomit again; and the sow that was washed to her wallowing in the mire."

The entire context that Peter covers in this chapter is the unrighteous, the ungodly, the false prophet, the false teacher in contrast with the righteous. He repeatedly states in various ways that they have been placed into darkness, spiritual blindness, and kept there until the day, the time, the age of judgment. It is totally out of context to bring "fallen angels" into the discussion at all. Due to the translation given by those translating from the Greek and due to the incorrect assumptions and teachings of most of Christianity we have failed to grasp and understand what Peter was telling us.

JUDE

We find an almost exact series of verses in the book of Jude. Jude is writing to those "sanctified by God the Father, and preserved in Jesus, and called:," verse 1. He says in verse 3 that it was needful for him to write unto them and exhort them "that ye should earnestly contend for the faith which was once delivered unto the saints." In verse 4 he begins his discussion by saying, "For there are certain men..." The context is men. He continues, "crept in unawares, who were before of old ordained to this condemnation, ungodly men,..." Much as Peter wrote he is speaking of the ungodly, unrighteous men. In verse 5 he continues to speak of men, "having saved the people out of the land of Egypt, afterward destroyed them that believed not."

Now we come to verse 6, which sounds almost like Peter's statement we just read in II Peter 2:4. "And the angels which kept not their first estate, but left their own habitation, he hath reserved in everlasting chains under darkness unto the judgement of the great day." The word translated "angels" is again *aggelos* or *angelos* and can be accurately rendered "messenger." Notice how Young's Literal Bible translates this verse, "messengers also, those who did not keep their own principality, but did leave their proper dwelling, to a judgement of a great day, in bonds everlasting, under darkness He hath kept." See the above explanation of chains, judgment.

Everlasting chains

But, one might ask, what about the "everlasting" chains? Doesn't that mean for all eternity? No! The Greek word translated "everlasting" is *aidios*. I'd like to quote a section from a book that I would recommend that thoroughly discusses the subject of "everlasting", "eternal", "forever", as used in Scripture. The book is titled "The Greek Word AION—AIONIOS, Translated Everlasting—Eternal in the HOLY BIBLE, Shown to Denote Limited Duration" and was written by John Wesley Hanson, copyrighted in 1875. Quoting from the Appendix of this book regarding the word *aidios*. "It is further admitted that the word is here used in the exact sense of *aionios*, as is seen in the succeeding verse: 'Even as Sodom and Gomorrah, and the cities about them in like manner, giving themselves over to fornication, and going after strange flesh, are set forth for an example, suffering the vengeance of eternal fire.' That is to say, the '*aidios*' chains in verse 6 are 'even as' durable as the '*aionion* fire' in verse 7. Which word modifies the other? The construction of the language shows that the latter word limits the former. The *aidios* chains are even as the *aionion* fire. As if one should say 'I have been infinitely troubled, I have been vexed for an hour,' or 'He is an endless talker, he can talk five hours on a stretch.' Now while 'infinitely' and 'endless' convey the sense of unlimited, they are both limited by what follow, as *aidios*, eternal, is limited by *aionios*, indefinitely long." Mr. Hanson also points out that the "everlasting" chains are limited by the fact it was to last only until "a judgment of a great day."

Speaks of men

Just as we saw in II Peter 2, the context here continues to speak of men. Verse 6, the people of Sodom and Gomorrha. Verse 8, speaks of "filthy dreamers." In verse 9 Jude tells us that there had been a contention between Michael and the adversary about the body of Moses and Michael dared not bring a railing accusation. He continues the thought in verse 10 by saying, "But these (the people, individuals he has been speaking about) speak evil of those things which they know not:..." Verse 11 he says they, these individuals, have gone the way of Cain, after the error of Balaam, and he says they "perished in the gainsaying of Core." Verse 12 continues, "These.." This is the same these, the people he has been discussing throughout the whole letter. He says they are spots, clouds without water, trees without fruit and verse 13, raging waves of the sea, wandering stars. He says, "to whom is reserved the blackness of darkness (we have discussed "darkness" above) for ever.

"Ever" is from the Greek *aion*, properly translated "age." (See the book referenced above for a very detailed and complete discussion.) Verse 14 says that Enoch prophesied of "these," the same these he has been discussing, unholy and unrighteous men. Verse 15 speaks of the judgment to be executed on the ungodly, the "these" he has been talking about. Verse 19 refers to verse 17 and 18 regarding the words which the apostles of Jesus had spoken regarding mockers in the last time that would walk after their own ungodly lusts. He says, verse 19, "These (the same these) be they...having not the Spirit."

Neither Peter or Jude speak of angelic beings sinning but of unrighteous and ungodly men. Due to unfortunate translation and pagan beliefs that crept in we have been taught error regarding these passages.

CHAPTER SEVEN

ORIGIN AND PURPOSE OF THE ADVERSARY

TERTULLIAN

Earlier we mentioned Tertullian and his teaching on Isaiah 14 and Lucifer. During my research I came across a copy of the doctrinal thesis of Robert E. Roberts D.D., written in 1924, almost 100 years ago. It was titled The Theology of Tertullian. In Chapter 6 there is a paragraph in which the devil is discussed.[8] "THE DEVIL---Concerning the origin and existence of the devil the ideas of Tertullian are clear and unmistakable. Basing his statement on an ingenious exposition of Ezek. xxviii, 11-16, which he makes to refer to the devil, he shows that God created an angel with free will. This angel was formed for good, but by his own choice became evil. 'He was once irreproachable at the time of his creation, formed for good by God as by the good Creator of irreproachable creatures, and adorned with every angelic glory, and associated with God, good with the Good, but afterwards of his own accord removed to evil.' The motive which led to his fall was his own lusting after the wickedness which was spontaneously conceived within him. This is more precisely indicated as envy, and malice, and impatience, prompted by the fact that God subjected

---

[8] https://www.tertullian.org/articles/roberts_theology/roberts_07.htm

the works which He made to man. The fall of the devil (or Satan) was from the heights of heaven, where he dwelt in the Paradise of God. Henceforth he became the adversary of God, and the author and instigator of evil and wickedness in men. He seduced the woman in the garden, and through her the man also. As he had misused his own free will, so he taught men to misuse theirs. Every manner of subtlety is employed by him to alienate men from God."

Dr. Roberts has given us Tertullian's teaching in a brief paragraph. It appears to be what is basically the general teaching today in most of Christianity. I believe that Dr. Robert's wording was intentional when he states in the second sentence of the paragraph that Tertullian based his teaching on an "ingenious exposition of Ezek." "Ingenious" is defined as "adroit, clever, cunning, inventive." Dr. Roberts is saying that the doctrine that came from Tertullian was very cleverly devised and invented.

But, just what is the truth? Where did the devil come from? The Bible gives us the answer, and it may surprise you. We have been taught our whole lives exactly what Tertullian and others put forth, and the adversary himself was behind it. He hasn't wanted us to truly see him for what he is, to understand his origin. Let us look at what the Word of God tells us.

GOD CREATED ALL THINGS

The Word tells us that **all things** were created by God, or more accurately by the one that became Jesus Christ. Notice what the Apostle Paul was inspired to write in Colossians 1:16-17. "For by him were all things created, that are in heaven, and that are in earth, visible and invisible, whether they be thrones or dominions, or principalities, or powers: all things were created by him, and for him: And he is before all things, and by him all things consist." There is nothing in existence that was not created by God. Paul specifically mentions dominions, principalities, and powers. This includes the adversary, the devil. Everything that exists had a beginning point. When God speaks of "the beginning" of anything, He is speaking of the originating point of the subject in question. The originating point is not the same for all things.

Webster's dictionary defines "beginning" as "(1) a start (2) the time or place of starting or coming into being; origin; source". I don't believe that any of us that have a basic working knowledge of the English language has any difficulty understanding the meaning of "in the beginning" or "from the beginning." The beginning of anything is simply the time or place of its starting or coming into being.

Let us read of one beginning. John 2:11, "This beginning of miracles did Jesus in Cana of Galilee, and manifested forth his glory; and his disciples believed on him." As I'm sure we understand, the miraculous aspect of Jesus' ministry had as its originating point this miracle of turning the water into wine at the marriage in Cana. He had not performed any miracles until that point in time. From that point many miracles were to follow. So far as His miracles were concerned this was "the beginning". Once something is manifested in a certain form "from the beginning" that means that from the time it was first formed, established, and came into being, it has been in that condition.

Genesis

The very first book in our Bibles is Genesis. Webster's dictionary defines "genesis", a Greek word meaning "origin, source, generation, or beginning" as "the way in which something comes to be, beginning, origin." The original Hebrew word for this book is *Bereshith* meaning "in the beginning". The book of Genesis reveals to us the beginning point or points in time of the origin of God's creation. As we said, not all things came into being, originated, or began at the exact same moment in time. Let us turn to the book of Genesis and notice that.

Genesis 1:1, "In the beginning God created the heaven and the earth." What we are told here is that there was a point in time (time pertains to the physical) that God created "the heaven and the earth". We aren't told exactly when this was. You may or may not know that there is a great deal of speculation and many theories as to when "the beginning" was. Some feel that it was millions, if not billions, of years ago. Some think that everything mentioned here in Genesis happened about 6000 years ago. Others believe the "gap theory," that there was a "gap" in time between verses one and two of Genesis chapter 1. It isn't within the scope of this book to pursue that. But, I think we all see and understand that what we have recorded for us here in Genesis is pertaining to the creation and preparation of the earth for mankind. God says He created everything mankind would need and then He ceased creating on the seventh day. Many of the things prepared for mankind during those seven days are outlined for us.

We are told that the plant life was brought into being. Fish and all aquatic life were created. Specifically mentioned is the creation of cattle and the beasts of the earth. The pinnacle of God's creation was the making of mankind in His image and His likeness. (Gen. 1:26-27) Chapter 2 of Genesis appears to be a second account of this creation. Here we see a few additional things that God created. We are told that He planted a garden in Eden and placed the man there. We find something very interesting in verse 9. We are told of two trees that God planted in the midst of this garden in addition to the trees that were for man's food. Those trees were the tree of life and the tree of knowledge of good and evil.

EVIL

Here is something else that was created and we aren't speaking of the tree. Evil was created since we are told that this tree was the tree of knowledge of good and evil. Did God create evil? We read a bit earlier in Colossians 1 that God created ALL things. And, yes He created evil! Notice, in case you have never seen this before, Isaiah 45:7, "I form the light, and create darkness: I make peace, and create evil: I the LORD do all these things." In the teaching most of us have received over the years we were told that it was "the devil" that rebelled against God and somehow devised and created evil. The devil never created anything. Read Colossians 1:16-17 again. God created ALL things, and that includes evil.

I can almost hear some of you saying, "But, God said that He saw all He had made and that it was very good, so how could He have created evil?" We need to take a moment or two and look at this. The Hebrew word translated "evil" is *ra'* or *ra'ah*, Strong's number H7451. This word is used both in Genesis 2:9 and in Isa. 45:7. As a matter of fact, this Hebrew word is used over 660 times in the Old Testament, and although "evil" is the primary way it is translated, it is also translated in over 40 other ways. The most often are "evil," "wickedness," "wicked," "hurt," "mischief," and "bad." Interestingly it is never translated "sin."

We may have never considered it, but if we never had to face evil, adversity, and difficulties we would never develop and build the Godly character God desires for us. Most probably don't believe that God knew before mankind was created that we would sin. We are told that God knows our frame, He knows how He made us. As we will see in a little bit, God created the adversary for that very purpose. We often think that all evil comes from the devil, but God says over and over that it is He that often brought evil. In the book of Jeremiah alone there are more than 30 verses that reference God either doing evil or repenting from evil which He had purposed doing. There are many similar passages in other books as well, but let us look at a verse in Jeremiah 11. You might want to start back a few verses but we'll just read verse 11, "Therefore thus saith the LORD, I will bring evil upon them, which they shall not be able to escape;" Did you notice that God doesn't say "I will **allow** evil to come upon them," but "I will **bring** evil upon them."

A brief answer to the question posed back a couple of paragraphs regarding God saying all was very good and how He could have created evil is found in Romans 8:28. It states that "all things" which would include any and all evil that might come our way, "work together for good to them that love God, to them who are the called according to his purpose." We'll look at this a bit more in depth as we go on, but He knew that even the evil would be used to accomplish the ultimate good.

THE SERPENT

Genesis 3:1 introduces us to another of God's creations, the serpent. In our King James Version of the Bible we read, "Now the serpent was more subtil than any beast of the field which the LORD God had made." Over the years commentators, scholars, and Bible students have pondered over what kind of an animal or beast that the adversary spoke through. I believe the way the verse has been translated has been a misdirection. We have viewed the phrase "which the LORD God had made" as modifying the "any beast of the field." Since the Hebrew doesn't contain any punctuation the modifier has been placed where the translators think it should go, based on their teaching. But, I believe the subject in this verse is "the serpent." If we punctuate this verse with the modifier where it should be it would be a bit clearer. Notice, "Now the serpent, (comma) which the LORD God had made, (comma) was more subtil than any beast of the field." We now have the emphasis upon God having made "the serpent."

Rather than trying to speculate on what kind of animal or beast the adversary spoke through (being a great ventriloquist) we see that he was "the serpent, the dragon" in his manifestation. This shouldn't be a surprise to us, as we see throughout the Bible angelic beings being described as animals. Take time to read the descriptions of the living creatures Ezekiel saw, Ezekiel chapter one. Look at verse 10, "As for the likeness of their faces, they four had the face of a man, and the face of a lion on the right side: and they four had the face of an ox on the left side; and they four also had the face of an eagle." When we look at what we read over in the book of Revelation, we see clearly that the being we call the adversary, the devil, is specifically called a serpent and a dragon (a fabulous kind of serpent, per Strong's definitions). Let us read Rev. 12:9, "And the great dragon was cast out, that old serpent, called the devil, and satan (adversary),which deceiveth the whole world:" (See also Rev. 20:2. He is again described in the same way.)

Hypocatastasis

The Bible uses numerous figures of speech. We are most familiar with similes and metaphors, but not so much so with the hypocatastasis. A simile draws a comparison or resemblance most often by the use of the comparative words "like" or "as." A metaphor makes the comparison by actual representation. "He is like a clumsy ox" is a simile. But, "He is a clumsy ox" is a metaphor. The hypocatastasis is where the comparison is by implication, it is only implied. In our example saying "ox" would be a hypocatastasis, since the subject of the comparison is only implied. Here in Genesis 3:1 "the serpent" comparison to the adversary is implied, thus a hypocatastasis. It is not speaking of a literal snake. That is just a fable that continues to be taught as fact.

Shining one

Serpent here in Genesis 3:1 is translated from the Hebrew word *nachash,* Strong's number H5175. The definition given by Dr. Strong is "snake, serpent." However, I found it interesting that Bullinger in The Companion Bible states that *nachash* is from a root word meaning "to shine" thus the meaning of *nachash* is "a shining one." The International Standard Version of the Bible translates Genesis 3:1 this way, "Now the shining one..." This would seem to fit with the apostle Paul's statement in 2 Corinthians 11:14, "And no marvel; for Satan (the adversary) is transformed into an angel of light."

Checking various commentaries and resources I came across a very interesting statement in the Treasury of Scriptural Knowledge (TSK)[9], "The Samaritan[10] copy, instead of *nachash,* 'a serpent,' reads *cachash* (or *kachash*), 'a liar or deceiver,' read John 8:44." The last part of John 8:44 says, "When he speaketh a lie, he speaketh of his own: for he is a liar, and the father of it."

---

[9] The Treasury of Scriptural Knowledge is a comprehensive, user-friendly Bible study tool with over 500,000 Scriptural references and contains one of the most exhaustive listing of biblical cross-references available. This is a collection of many authors work over many centuries.

[10] Samaritan Pentateuch The Samaritans accepted only the Pentateuch, the Torah, or "the Law." The manuscript from which it was derived appears to be somewhat different from that which was used by the Jews. There are important differences between the Hebrew and the Samaritan copies in the reading of many sentences. In about 2000 instances in which they disagree the Septuagint agrees with the Samaritan. The New Testament when quoting from the Old Testament agrees as a rule with the Samaritan. Many of the differences are spelling differences. In some cases the Samaritan includes a bit more information.

Not being a Hebrew scholar I can't say if either of these explanations are accurate but they do both fit with the Scriptures. I found one additional comment that we might want to consider, again I can't say whether this individual has it correct or not. He stated that the word *nachash* we have been looking at could be a noun, or a verb, or an adjective, depending on the usage. His comment was that as a noun it means "serpent." As a verb it means to "divine". But, as an adjective it would mean "shining," or "the shining one."

THE BEGINNING OF THE SERPENT

We have looked at and discussed the fact that the adversary was not an archangel that rebelled and became the evil one. We saw that ALL things were created by the Creator God, including this being. As we saw, God says that He created evil. The adversary did not create anything. He is evil because God made him that way. Earlier we discussed "beginnings." When was the beginning of this being? Wonder no more. The Bible tells us.

We have referred to John 8:44 previously but let us look at it again. Jesus is speaking, verse 42. Then in verse 44 He says, "Ye are of your father the devil, and the lusts of your father ye will do." Jesus is being very plain in His statement to these Jews. He tells them that the devil is their father. Notice what He says as He continues. "He (the devil) was a murderer from the beginning, and abode not in the truth, because there is no truth in him." Jesus speaks here of the beginning of the adversary, the devil. From the beginning, He says, the devil was a murderer. Look at what He says further as we continue reading this passage. "When he speaketh a lie, he speaketh of his own: for he is a liar, and the father of it." In this one verse we are told by Jesus when the beginning of the devil was. From his beginning he was a murderer and a liar. When was that?

We have been looking at Genesis 3 and verse 1. We hadn't come to the last part of the verse. Here we are told of the exchange between the serpent and the woman. This continues on through the next several verses. In verse 4 we read the first recorded lie, a statement totally opposite of what God had said, "And the serpent said unto the woman, Ye shall not surely die." Remember what Jesus said, "From the beginning." Due to his lie the woman and the man disobeyed God and, as God had told them, death entered. The adversary was a murderer and a liar from the beginning.

As a matter is established in the mouth of two or three witnesses let us look at one more scripture, 1 John 3:8. "He that committeth sin is of the devil; for the devil sinneth from the beginning." This passage is again speaking of the devil's beginning. Continuing, "For this purpose the Son of God was manifested, that he might destroy the works of the devil." The adversary wasn't created holy and after eons of time rebelled and became the devil. From his very beginning he was sinning, missing the mark, transgressing God's holy laws. When was this? We just read of that event in Genesis chapter 3.

Let us rehearse what we have looked at. During the creation week, summarized in Genesis chapters 1 and 2, we saw that God created everything that mankind would ever need. He ceased creating, He rested, on the seventh day as everything mankind would ever need was provided for. And, one of the things mankind would need, which we don't seem to ever think about, was adversity and difficulties. Without facing adversity, evil, and difficulties, mankind would have been nothing but a robot or an automaton. To develop Godly character there is a need to face and overcome trials and tests. Even in the natural world we often speak of the "survival of the fittest". Those that face and overcome the challenges are the ones that survive. Plants raised in a greenhouse may look robust but moved out where they are met with wind, rain, and other challenging events they will die.

THE SERPENT WORKS FOR GOD

Recently, I was reading a short article written by a church pastor and Bible school professor. He made a statement that I had to take exception to. He said, "The devil doesn't work for God." I understand that all of us have been under the adversary's deception, and the common teaching is that the devil is actively striving to thwart God's plan for mankind. But, far from it. He is doing exactly what God made him to do. We'll look at some examples from the Word and we'll notice some things that most of us have never seen before. As we talked about in the last paragraph we need adversity, consequently there is a need for an adversary. God provided for all of our needs, even our need for adversity.

God, the adversary, and Job

Most of us are familiar with the story of Job. What most of us have been taught is that Job had a major problem, he was self-righteous. When I was in college one of my Bible classes was given the assignment to write a paper on the subject of "Job and me." It was to be a self examination by each student into their own issue with self-righteousness. Again, we were in deception. The Bible never tells us that Job was self-righteous. Notice what God had to say about Job, Job 1:8, "And the LORD said unto Satan (the adversary), Hast thou considered my servant Job, that there is none like him in the earth, a perfect and an upright man, one that feareth God, and escheweth evil?" Not self-righteous but a perfect and an upright man. When we come to chapter 2 we see that God repeats what He had said, Job 2:3, "And the LORD said unto Satan (the adversary), Hast thou considered my servant Job, that there is none like him in the earth, a perfect and an upright man, one that feareth God, and escheweth evil?"

Perhaps we have not seen what was going on in the account. In chapter 1 and verse 7 we read of God speaking to the adversary and asking him what he had been doing. The adversary responds that he had been going about his business, going to and fro in the earth, and from walking up and down in it. Then God asks the adversary, as we just read in verse 8, if he had considered Job. The adversary basically says that there wasn't any need for him to come against Job because God had made a hedge around him and his house and all that he had. God didn't dispute this, but let us notice what He tells the adversary, verse 12, "Behold, all that he hath is in thy power; only upon himself put not forth thine hand." Just as a person might sic his dog onto another dog or some other animal God is sicing the adversary on Job.

Following this we read of all the evil that the adversary brings upon Job. We find that in the face of all of this Job fell down and worshiped God (verse 20) and "In all this Job sinned not, nor charged God foolishly." (verse 22) In chapter 2 we read of another encounter God had with the adversary. After asking what the adversary had been doing we find that once again God asks if he, the adversary, had considered Job. The adversary tells God that Job is holding to his integrity because he hasn't been allowed to attack him bodily. What did God do? Once again he says "Sic him!" Verse 6, "Behold, he is in thine hand; but save his life." Most of us know the story of Job's three "friends" who try to convince Job that he obviously has sin in his life. But, Job remains faithful to God.

Why, we may be asking, did God not only allow the adversary to do all of the evil things he did but actually sent him to do them? Job was given revelation as to why. It is the same reason all of us go through many different trials, tests, temptations, and evil. We find the answer in Job's own words, Job 23:10, "But he knoweth the way that I will take: when he hath tried me, I shall come forth as gold." Job was perfect, as we read earlier, but he had not been tried. His perfection remained to be proven, tested, and demonstrated. The Scriptures state that God searches the reins of the heart, knows who can be trusted with affliction, tries the righteous, and will not allow any to be tested beyond what they are able to bear. We won't take the time to go through all of it here but you should read the last five chapters of the book of Job.

God has a conversation with Job. At the conclusion of all that God had to tell him Job had not only passed the test but all had turned out for good as we read in Romans 8:28. Job had a much deeper understanding and relationship with God. God blessed him physically with much more than he had at the beginning of this trial.

But, one thing I want us to notice. We have seen that it was the adversary that did all of the terrible things to Job at God's direction. That is brought out in the last chapter of the book, chapter 42 and verse 11, "...and comforted him over all the evil (*ra* or *ra'ah*) that the LORD had brought upon him:" (emphasis mine) Yes, God created evil and does evil to accomplish good in the end.

Paul's thorn in the flesh

Much has been taught and written about Paul's thorn in the flesh. The most common teaching is that Paul had some kind of terrible eye disease. Some have gone so far as to declare that he had eyes that were matted and full of pus, that he was practically blind. That is not what we find from this passage of Scripture. The verse that states that Paul had a thorn in the flesh is 2 Corinthians 12:7. Not only do various commentators put forth the explanation we have just talked about but even some translations of the Bible give us that understanding, which, as we will see, is false. The Good News Bible states "I was given a painful physical ailment." This is not a translation but the personal belief of the one doing the "translation" work.

There are quite a number of commentators and teachers that do see that Paul tells us that this "thorn" he was dealing with was "the messenger of Satan (the adversary)." But, few give the explanation that Paul gives us. One of the rules of proper Bible study is to look at and consider the context of the item, phrase, or statement in question. That is what we will take a bit of time to look at. Keep in mind that there were no chapter breaks in the original. Those have been added by the scholars and translators over the centuries. In most cases they are most likely in the best places but we shouldn't let them get in the way of following the context. We'll quickly follow the context through. I won't quote every word here as you can follow the story in your own Bible.

It can be difficult at times to know just where to begin, but I believe we can grasp what we are being told if we go up to 2 Corinthians 11 and begin at verse 16. The translators have felt that this is a new paragraph. Paul tell us he is perhaps being a bit foolish but is going to boast a bit. He does tell us in verse 17 that what he is going to share is "not after the LORD" but is his own foolish boasting. In verse 18 he says he knows that many "glory," or boast, as this could be translated. He continues by saying that he "will glory (or boast) also." In verses 19, 20, and 21 Paul seems to be a bit sarcastic. He indicates that they, the Corinthians, seem to put up with those that are truly fools. He says that he, Paul, is bold as some of these foolish ones were.

Paul begins to ask them about these individuals they put up with. He asks if they are Hebrews and ministers of Christ. (verses 22 and 23) At this point Paul begins to enumerate all of the things that he has endured. You can read through all of them, but he mentions being beaten, being stoned, being shipwrecked, and many other things. He alludes to much more when he mentions the perils or dangers he faced everywhere. Beginning with verse 29 he starts to give us a bit more of the real story. He speaks of being weak and then in verse 30 he states, "If I must needs glory (or boast), I will glory (or boast) of the things which concern mine infirmities." Some might assume that he is speaking of sicknesses when he says "infirmities." As Vine's states, the Greek carries the meaning of "weaknesses."

In verse 31 Paul throws in the fact that in all he is recounting he is not lying. In verses 32 and 33 he tells of his escape from the city of Damascus. Ignoring the chapter break, we continue with verse 1 of chapter 12 in our Bibles. He says it most likely is not profitable to be boasting. He says he will move on to visions and revelations. With verses 2 through 5 he speaks of one, and most assume he is speaking of himself, being taken up to the third heaven, whether in reality or in a vision he says he really didn't know. He states in verse 4 that what was heard was "unspeakable words, which it is not lawful for a man to utter." Many believe that he was told he couldn't share what he had heard with anyone.

In verse 5 he states that he would glory of the one that had been caught up but he would not glory or boast of any great things he had done, but his boasting would be in his infirmities or weaknesses. He states in verse 6 that should he desire to boast he was not going to be a fool. He was going to speak the truth. Now we come to verse 7, the verse that has sparked so much debate and many discussions and statements. Let us read this verse, and then we'll look at what it says and doesn't say.

"And lest I should be exalted above measure through the abundance of the revelations, there was given to me a thorn in the flesh, the messenger of Satan (the adversary) to buffet me, lest I should be exalted above measure." There are some other translations that make this verse much clearer. The Weymouth translation is one, "And judging by the stupendous grandeur of the revelations—therefore lest I should be over-elated there has been sent to me, like the agony of impalement, Satan's angel dealing blow after blow, lest I should be over-elated."

Paul is telling us that he was human enough to become vain and prideful over what he had been given in revelation. The messenger was sent to him to continually, blow after blow, beat him down to keep him from becoming proud, exalted, and conceited (as other translations render this). Let us continue with the next couple of verses. "For this thing (referring back to the messenger) I besought the LORD thrice, that it might depart from me." (verse 8) Now look at God's response, verse 9, "And he said unto me, My grace is sufficient for thee: for my strength is made perfect in weakness. Most gladly therefore will I rather glory (boast) in my infirmities (weaknesses), that the power of Christ may rest upon me."

In the next verses Paul states that he takes pleasure in the weaknesses, reproaches, persecutions, and distresses that he suffered for Christ's sake. He recognized that when he was at his weakest he was made strong through Christ. He said that he had become a fool in his bragging.

One thing we read over and didn't hone in on was the statement Paul made in verse 7, "there was given unto me." The word from which "given" is translated means just that, given. It isn't "allowed" or "permitted." Who gave him the thorn? God! The messenger, the angel of the adversary, was given the job of coming against Paul, buffeting him, dealing blow after blow. As other translations state, he was there to torment and harass Paul. He was given the job of pounding away at Paul. It was to accomplish the job of keeping Paul from becoming prideful and exalted. We saw earlier how God Himself sent the adversary against Job. In this case it wasn't as much about trying and testing Paul as it was to keep him in constant recognition of his own weakness and the need for the strength that came from Jesus.

We are continuing to see that it was God who made the serpent, the adversary, and his angels to come against mankind. The adversary is doing what he was created to do, bringing adversity into the lives of each of us. Again, all things work together for good to those who love God and are called according to His purpose. (Rom.8:28)

JESUS AND THE WILDERNESS

Matthew, Mark, and Luke give us a brief account of Jesus' encounter with the adversary in the wilderness. As significant as this time was we are only given 26 verses of Scripture telling us of it. Most of us have heard and read these passages and know that Jesus spent 40 days and nights totally fasting. In His most weakened state physically He is tempted by the adversary. Jesus was prepared for the temptation. Fasting was not to go without food but was to totally deny the flesh, the body, and to draw as close as possible to the Father for the spiritual strength needed. We can all be eternally thankful that Jesus came out victorious. But, one thing that many have never taken notice of is the fact that God the Father sent Him out into the wilderness to face the adversary.

We need to take note of what each writer tells us. Turn in your own Bible and look at these statements. Matt. 4:1, "Then was Jesus led up of the Spirit into the wilderness to be tempted of the devil." It was God, by the Holy Spirit, that took Jesus out there to face the adversary. Mark, in his very brief account of only two verses, tells us the same thing. Mark 1:12, "And immediately (following Jesus' baptism by John and receiving the Holy Spirit) the Spirit driveth him into the wilderness." Verse 13 tells us the purpose was for Him to be tempted of the adversary. Luke uses the same words that Matthew used, Luke 4:1, "And Jesus being full of the Holy Ghost returned from Jordan, and was led by the Spirit into the wilderness." He continues to tell us that the purpose was for Jesus to be tempted of the devil (verse 2).

God, the Father, by the Holy Spirit, led or drove Jesus out into that wilderness to be tempted by the adversary. Jesus didn't just decide to go out there, nor was it just the adversary's idea that he dreamed up, but it was the job he had been given. Following the "fall" in the garden it was prophesied that the woman's seed, Jesus, would be attacked by the serpent. Genesis 3:15 says that the serpent would "bruise his heel," or attack Jesus in His human body. But, the positive side was that "it (literally 'he,' the seed, Jesus) shall bruise thy head." Jesus was prophesied to be victorious.

I think that we sometimes think that this temptation was the only time Jesus had to face the adversary. But, no, Jesus was harassed, tried, and tempted throughout His ministry. Many times it was the religious leaders who were being used by the adversary. Luke tells us in his account of Jesus' temptation in the wilderness that "he (the devil) departed from him for a season." (Luke 4:13) For a season indicates "until an opportune time" or until another opportunity presented itself. Of course, the greatest trial came at the last 40 hours of Jesus' physical life when He was arrested, mistreated, scourged, and finally crucified. (For a detailed timeline of those 40 hours see Chapter 10 in my book Shadows of Jesus in the Exodus.) All of this was for our benefit at the Father's direction. Jesus prayed to the Father that if there was any other way to let it be, but, He replied that not His will but that it be the Father's will. (See Matt. 26:39; Mark 14:35-36; Luke 22:42)

In the next chapter we will look at how the adversary is doing his job as it applies to each of us. What he is doing is at the direction and the plan of God. The devil is not a "fallen archangel" that has gone rogue. He was made, created by God and given a job to do.

CHAPTER EIGHT

YOU AND ME AND THE ADVERSARY

At this point I have to believe we have discussed most of the erroneous teachings and beliefs extant about the adversary, the devil. I apologize if I've missed some. However, I want to spend a bit of time looking at what you and I face as believers and how we need to deal with those things.

GODLY SHALL SUFFER PERSECUTION

The apostle Paul, writing to the young evangelist Timothy, states in 2 Tim. 3:12, "Yea, and all that will live godly in Christ Jesus shall suffer persecution." One of the definitions of "persecution" given by Thayer's Greek dictionary is "in any way to harass, trouble, molest one." We can expect to be troubled and harassed because of our beliefs. Persecution may come in many forms, and it doesn't come from God but from the one that has been given the job, the adversary. Paul addresses believers in his epistles as saints, holy, sanctified, justified, redeemed, righteous, the elect of God. That is our identity in Christ. But, just as Job was brought to see, Job 23:10, we need to be tried that we also may "come forth as gold."

James, writing to the twelve tribes and to those addressed as brethren, tells us that blessings follow adversity. Let us read his statement in the first chapter of the book of James, verse 12, "Blessed is the man that endureth temptation: for when he is tried, he shall receive the crown of life, which the LORD hath promised to them that love him." One of Strong's definitions of "temptation" is adversity. By the adversity we are "tried," or are proved. Once again the purpose is that we "come forth as gold."

In the previous chapter we reviewed briefly the wilderness temptation of Jesus. We might ask, "Do we have to go through the same kinds of temptations and trials that Jesus went through?" Actually it is the reverse. Jesus had to go through the same kinds of trials and temptations that you and I must go through. Let us look at Hebrews 4:15. Speaking here of Jesus who was made our High Priest, "For we have not an high priest which cannot be touched with the feeling of our infirmities; but was in all points tempted like as we are, yet without sin." He became flesh, was human, and He dealt with the same trials and temptations that we have been given to deal with. Why was that? Back a couple of chapters we are given the answer. Heb. 2:18, "For in that he himself suffered being tempted, he is able to succour them that are tempted." Having experienced what we face Jesus in His love and compassion is very able to provide the help we need to deal with what comes at us.

The apostle Paul, writing to the church at Corinth, made a statement that I'm not sure we could all personally say and truly mean it. In

2 Cor. 2:11 Paul says, "Lest Satan (the adversary) should get an advantage of us: for we are not ignorant of his devices." Perhaps we all are still a bit ignorant of just how the adversary comes at us. We have looked at a number of verses that tell us that he is a deceiver, a liar, a murderer. Jesus told us exactly what the adversary is doing. Notice John 10:10, "The thief cometh not, but for to steal, and to kill, and to destroy:" But, as we read in Genesis 3:1, when the serpent was made, he was "more subtil" than any beast. Subtil is described as cunning, crafty, and shrewd. Many times, if not most of the time, we can be totally unaware of his schemes. We are told something and if it sounds good we never question whether it is truth from God or one of the adversary's lies. He can be a super salesman. He has been in "marketing" from that beginning. If we aren't on our toes, so to speak, he can convince us of why we "need" what he is selling. In Hebrews 11 we are told that Moses made the choice "to suffer affliction with the people of God, than to enjoy the pleasures of sin for a season." (Heb. 11:25) Sin can be pleasurable and the adversary knows which of our buttons to push.

He may throw things at us that our brothers and sisters never have to deal with. Why? He knows us pretty well and knows what and how to get to us. He will attempt to exploit any character flaw or weakness we may have. Do we need to live in fear that he is going to somehow get us "off track"? No! We need to recognize our identity in Christ, believe that we have been given power and authority by Jesus, and walk in it. Notice that Jesus told the seventy (who weren't even born again and in possession of the Holy Spirit) that they were given "power to tread on serpents and scorpions, and over all the power of the enemy:"

(Luke 10:19, emphasis mine.) We have been given that power and authority. We need to recognize that and learn to use it.

James tells us, chapter 4 and verse 7, "Resist the devil, and he will flee from you." How do we resist? The first part of that same verse tells us, "Draw nigh to God, and he will draw nigh to you." This is what we saw with Jesus in His wilderness temptation. He used the tool of fasting and prayer to draw as close as possible to God, His Father. The second part of His being able to resist the adversary was in His knowing the Word, the Scriptures. He knew them and was able to recognize the twist the adversary attempted to put on passages he quoted. Peter also tells us to resist the adversary, the devil. (1Pet. 5:8) When you read the context (verses 5-9), he speaks of how that is accomplished. He speaks repeatedly of humbling ourselves, being clothed with humility. He states that we need to be sober and vigilant. These are all a part of "drawing nigh to God."

He tells us why we need to be doing this. "Because your adversary the devil, as a roaring lion, walketh about seeking whom he may devour." (verse 8) A "roaring lion" isn't approaching the prey with stealth. He is looking for the weak and vulnerable. By roaring he is attempting to instill fear. We, if we are drawing near to God and humbling ourselves before Him, have no fear. We know our identity and know the power and authority we have been given.

Paul, in the concluding chapter of the book of Ephesians, tells us plainly who our adversary is and how we must deal with him. Chapter 6 and beginning with verse 11 we are told of the armour we need to stand against the "wiles of the devil." Verse 12 lets us know that we are in a wrestling match but not with a physical opponent. Our opponents are the adversary and his angels. Paul tells us they are "principalities," "powers," "rulers of the darkness of this world," "spiritual wickedness in high places." He enumerates the various aspects of the armour we are to put on. You can read, study, and meditate on all of these items, verses 14-18. The concluding two things are central to all of the items, knowing the Word of God and our relationship with God through prayer.

The adversary, that old serpent, the devil, is real. He has been given a job to do and he is good at it. We need to expect his attempts upon us, but we can have confidence in the power and authority of Jesus Christ that we have been given. We can't be lackadaisical and assume he can't get to us. Let us draw close to God and resist the devil. Let each of us declare, along with Job, "when he hath tried me, I shall come forth as gold." (Job 23:10)

This is not the end of the story, but as far as we will go for now. To be answered is the question of what happens to the adversary. What is his future? Most of us have read the Scripture that tells us that he is to be bound for 1000 years and then loosed for a little while. Then what? The answer might surprise you. To share it at this point would require perhaps another book or two to dig through many more false teachings. So, until later!

ABOUT THE AUTHOR

Garry D. Pifer has been a reader and student of the Bible for over sixty years. In the mid-nineties he embarked on a much more diligent study. He wrote most of his studies in article form, many being put onto the internet and some published in an independent journal. In 2020 he authored **God's Bestseller: Make It Real In Your Life!** This book is a handbook giving a step by step guide to studying the Bible, giving the reader the benefit of what he had learned over 25 years. Led by the Holy Spirit he has donated over 2400 copies to prisons and jails across America.

Garry and his wife, Connie, have been married for fifty-nine years. They are the parents of four grown children. They have eleven grandchildren and five great-grandchildren. They currently reside in South-Central Kentucky.

Garry may be contacted by writing to him at P. O. Box 131, Edmonton, KY 42129 or by E-mail: gdpifer@scrtc.com

Other Books by Garry D. Pifer

God's Bestseller: Make It Real in Your Life!

Many have often wanted to understand the Bible but just thought it was a very confusing and closed book. In this conversational and straightforward book, Garry D. Pifer presents a step by step guide that will take you from a lack of understanding and a place of confusion to an opening up of what God has hidden FOR you, not from you. This book will give you direction in your search of the Scriptures. You will find priceless riches and treasures of great price. Read this book and learn how to find what has been concealed.

Shadows of Jesus in the Exodus

Most have not grasped the numerous shadows in the Egyptian Passover and of the exodus of the Israelites from Egypt that have their fulfillment in the final days of Jesus, His death, burial, and resurrection. This study takes you through the many details of the exodus, establishing the timeline of the events and moves onto the New Testament where the same timeline is revealed in the events of Jesus' final days and hours. Surprisingly you will find that many of the events did not occur on the days most Christians have been told that they happened. For an exciting study get and read Shadows of Jesus in the Exodus.

The History of Tithing: Where Are We Today?

The doctrine of tithing 10% of one's income is taught in almost every church. Where and when did tithing begin and what was tithed upon and to whom did it belong? Are we as new covenant believers under the command to tithe? For the complete history of tithing and whether it applies to you and me please obtain and read The History of Tithing: Where Are We Today?

Why Aren't Christians the Healthiest People on Earth?

It seems that most Christians believe that God exists and that He is all powerful. Most believe that He is able to heal all sicknesses and diseases but they are not sure that He will. Some believe that He brings sickness upon us to teach us lessons. Almost everyone appears to believe that God has given us the medical system for our health and healing and many aren't sure that divine healing is happening today. **Why Aren't Christians the Healthiest People on Earth?** looks at these beliefs and more. Garry D. Pifer will share his journey in the study of divine healing, looking at what the Bible reveals. What he discovered in his study may be totally contrary to what you have been taught and have believed from childhood. This challenging and thought provoking book can be read in one or two sittings but may lead to weeks and months of study and examination on your part.

These books are available from Amazon and other major booksellers.

www.ingramcontent.com/pod-product-compliance
Lightning Source LLC
Chambersburg PA
CBHW072213070526
44585CB00015B/1324